CW00505334

HIGHLIGHT
Intermediate
Student's Book

Michael Vince

Heinemann

Heinemann English Language Teaching
A division of Heinemann Publishers (Oxford) Ltd
Halley Court, Jordan Hill, Oxford OX2 8EJ

OXFORD   MADRID   ATHENS
PARIS   FLORENCE   PRAGUE   SÃO PAULO
CHICAGO   MELBOURNE   AUCKLAND   SINGAPORE
TOKYO   IBADAN   GABORONE   JOHANNESBURG
PORTSMOUTH (NH)

ISBN 0 435 28630 7
© Michael Vince 1992
First published 1992

All rights reserved; no part of this publication may be reproduced, stored in a retrieval system, or transmitted in any form or by any means, electronic, mechanical, photocopying, recording, or otherwise, without the prior permission of the Publishers.

Designed by Ron Kamen, Green Door Design Ltd
Cover photography by Ben Campbell
Illustrations by Mike Allport, Phil Burrows, Nick Duffy, Jeff Edwards, Belinda Evans, Alan Fraser, Geoff Jones, Ken Kirkland, Matthew Lawrence, Colin Mier, Anne Moorey, Morse, Linda Schwabs, Lyne Willey, Willow, Jo Wright.

Author Acknowledgements

Thanks to teachers in Spain, France, Greece and the U.K. who used or commented on earlier versions of these materials. Special thanks to Tanya Whatling and my sister Susan Lewis for authentic texts, and to students and colleagues at the Centre for English Language and Training, Athens for stimulation and support.

Text Acknowledgements

We would like to thank the following for their permission to reproduce a text:
Bella Magazine, for extracts from 'York, City of Living History' by Sarah Colliery (8 Apr 1989) p58; 'Rebels Without a Pause' by Jan Etherington (27 May 1989) pp67 and 68; 'Couples by Computer' by Nora McGrath (27 May 1989) p85; 'Ego Booster' by Andrew McKenna (11 Mar 1989) p76; *Best Magazine*, for 'Living With a Yugo 45A GLS' (4 Nov 1988) p41; British Telecom, for 'How to Use a Phonecard', p49; Harmsworth Publications Ltd, for 'Inhale and Hearty' from *Weekend* (26 November 1988) p50; *The Independent*, for text and photograph from '£40,000 to Take a Bus Home' by Stephen Ward (6 August 1988) p104; *Just 17*, for a Cartoon by Cathy Balme (16 Nov 1988) p86 and an extract from 'One Make-up Artist's Day' from 'Job File' by Eleanor Rodger (11 Sep 1988) p13; Times Newspapers Ltd, text from 'Boat Trip Terror as Petrol Runs Out', *Times Newspapers* (24 August 1988) p22; *TV Times*, for extract from 'Sting and the Children Who Sing for a Better World' by Lulu Appleton (25 Apr 1989) p94, programme extracts (3 Mar 1989) p93.

Photograph Acknowledgements

We would like to thank the following for their permission to reproduce photographs:
AA Picture Library p58 (tr), p59, p62 (bl, t) p101 (t, b); Allsport p73; Anglia Films/Tim Pigott-Smith, Karen Archer p93 (t); Aquarius Library p93 (t); Barnaby's Picture Library p5 (David Simson) (b), p10 (Richard Gardener) (t); Mary Evans Picture Library p3 (r); Format p73 (Sue de Jong) (t); Paul Freestone p67 (t), p100 (t); French Picture Library p62 (Barrie Smith) (t); Granada Television/Julie Goodyear, Roy Baraclough p93 (t); Ronald Grant p95; Houses and Interiors p100 (l, mr), p107 (t, t); The Hulton-Deutsch Collection p3 (1), p5 (ml), p47 (r); ITN p93 (t); J S Library p47 (r); Metropolitan Police p10 (t); Erik Pelham p1, p4 (t), p18 (airline tickets courtesy of BA) (t), p28, p29, p32, p35 (courtesy of R & S Webster, W.S. Surplus Supplies Ltd), p55, p57, p91 (poster courtesy of English National Ballet; theatre programme: The Playhouse, Oxford); Brian Phipps p67 (l); Photo-coop p10 (Julia Martin) (t), p67 (Gina Glover) (t); Photographer's Library p67 (t), p85; Popperfoto p40, p66, p75; Redferns p21 (m); Sarah Saunders p41; Scope Features, photograph 'Sting and the Children' by Michael Brennan p94; Tony Stone Photo Library p2 (Howard Grey), p4 (Chris Craymer) (b), p10 (Bruno de Hogues) (t), (Browne, Smee) (t); Topham p5 (m), p73 (© Homer Sykes) (tl); York City Council p58 (b1); Yugo Cars p41; Zefa p10 (t), p48, p62, (t, t, t), p73 (m), p107 (t).

Key t=top   b=bottom   m=middle   r=right   l=left

Typeset by Tradespools Ltd, Frome, Somerset

Printed and bound in Spain by Mateu Cromo, S.A. Pinto (Madrid)

94 95 96 10 9 8 7 6 5

CONTENTS MAP

CONTENTS MAP

Unit 1 The way we are

Getting to know each other

1 You have just met these two people, and you want to get to know them better. Make a list of questions you can ask them about the topics in the pictures.

2 Fill in this form about yourself, but do not show it to others.

Personal Details

1	The time you usually get up, and usually go to sleep.	_____
2	Two kinds of food that you like.	_____
3	Two unusual things you have got at home.	_____
4	Your favourite colour.	_____
5	How you come to lessons.	_____
6	Something you have got in your pocket or bag.	_____
7	The name of the last film you saw.	_____
8	Someone you admire.	_____
9	Your pet, if you have one.	_____
10	Your age last birthday.	_____

HAVE YOU GOT A PET?

3 Find other people in the class with the same answers. Introduce yourself and ask them questions.

1

▶ Customs and habits
▶ Past and present

1 Read the information below. Talk about customs and lifestyles in your country.

Strange But True ...

Customs

● In some parts of Britain, when a family moves house they take burning coals from the fire to the new house.
● Some people never throw egg-shells onto a fire. They believe that chickens stop laying eggs if you do this.
● Actors never whistle, and never say the last line of a play before they act it in public.

Lifestyles

● The Hadzas, a people in Central Africa, work for two hours a day finding food and spend the rest of the time enjoying themselves.
● Thirty million Americans eat too much and over eleven million Americans weigh more than 130 kilos.
● The British are great animal lovers and own more than six million cats.

Customs and lifestyles

Present simple   1.1

*The Hadzas **work** for two hours a day.*

Frequency adverbs   1.2

*Actors **never whistle**.*

See Grammar Reference p109

---

2 Ask a partner these questions.

SOCIAL CUSTOMS

In your country do people usually . . .
● shake hands when they meet someone or kiss them?
● give presents when they visit someone or on their birthday?
● use special words when talking to strangers, important people, or children?
● move their hands and heads a lot when they talk?
● eat special food on special days?
● wear special clothes on special occasions?

3 Find out about your partner's daily routines and habits.

Habitual activities

Present simple   1.1

*I **usually get up** at six.*
*I **sometimes play** tennis after work.*
*I **never drink** tea in the morning.*

4 How much do you know about the past? How did people live in the times shown in the pictures? Think about these points:

everyday activities   food and clothes   home and work

Past habits

Past simple   2.1

*People **went to bed** early.*

Used to   2.3
*People **used to read aloud** to one another.*

1

2

Did the same things happen a hundred years ago? Ask other people for their opinions and complete the table.

LIFESTYLES	
nowadays People spend a lot of time watching television in the evening. Women and men often share the housework and women have important jobs. People travel widely and often live and work far away from where they were born. Machines do many jobs, both in the home and at work. Most people spend more than ten years at school.	**in the past**

5 Make notes about yourself. Use your notes to describe the way you were in the past, and the way you are now.

	ten years ago	now
work/studies		
leisure activities		
likes/dislikes		
clothes		

3

SKILLS: READING AND LISTENING

Pre-reading

1 Are clothes important to you? Do you follow fashions? Which of the clothes in the list do you like?

jeans   tracksuit   hat   t-shirt
waistcoat boots   trainers mini-skirt

Describe the clothes you usually wear.

2 Read these statements about clothes. Which ones do you agree with?

a *I have to dress in a way which I can afford.*
b *I choose my clothes so I can follow the fashion in the music world.*
c *I like to be in fashion and love expensive things.*
d *I don't really care what other people think about my clothes.*
e *I have to be well-dressed so that I make a good impression on people.*
f *I think it is best to have smart, expensive clothes.*
g *I wear clothes which go with what I do, that's all.*
h *I dress the same as my friends, and not to look like anyone famous.*

1

2

Reading

3 Read the texts below. How do these people feel about clothes?

Feelings for Fashion

1 **Julie**   *My work affects the way I dress a great deal. I have to look good because I deal with directors, manufacturers, business people of all ages. In a*
5 *way, I have to sell myself as well as a product. I spend a fortune on clothes — about £1,500 each year.*

Paul   *I like pop music, but it annoys me when people say I am a fan of some*
10 *group just because my Levis are torn. That's simply the way I like to look. A lot of my friends dress like this, but to be more individual I sometimes wear old waistcoats and a hat.*

15 **Louise**   *During the day I have to wear a sort of school uniform, and the rules say it's got to be a horrible dark blue, but most evenings when I go dancing I wear the latest style, which for*
20 *now is trainers and a tracksuit with gold accessories. My gold bracelet cost £500 and my chain was £200. I think*

this is the real me.

Anna   *Once people went to clubs*
25 *just to get dressed up and meet someone. Now the thing is to sweat and dance all night. I wear as little as possible to keep cool, mainly loose-fitting T-shirts and trousers. I tie back my hair*
30 *and let myself go. But the music's the most important thing.*

Luke   *I often wear second-hand clothes from jumble sales, partly because as an art student I can't afford*
35 *anything else, but also because it is still quite fashionable. Though I think it is more 'in' to look smart now.*

Kate   *I always wear these old boots, it's a way of saying that I don't care*
40 *what most people think. I usually wear mini-skirts for cycling, not to be sexy but just because they're more practical than a long skirt, though I usually wear dirty jeans most of the time.*

Comprehension check

4 Which person in question 3:
  a is still at school?
  b is studying at college?
  c has an important job?
  d buys clothes which are not new?

Word search

5 a How much money is a fortune? A lot, or a little?
  b What verb does *torn* come from? What else can be torn?
  c What other people wear a uniform?
  d Where do you wear a bracelet?
  e Why does Anna need to keep cool?
  f Why is a mini-skirt more practical for cycling?

Speaking

6 What other kinds of clothes do the people in question 3 probably wear? Choose from the clothes in the list and explain your choices.

baseball cap
anorak
leather jacket
suit
high heeled shoes
long dress
fur coat
tie
sandals
shorts

Pre-listening

7 Do you like these fashions? When were they popular?

1

2

3

Listening

8 🖭 Listen to people talking about some of the fashions in question 7. Complete the table below.

	name of style	date	like/dislike
Graham		1950's	
Sarah			
Alec			

Which style do you like best?

GRAMMAR PRACTICE

Present simple ▶ 1.1

1 Here are some of the things that happen every hour in the world. Put one of the verbs from the list (in a suitable form) into the space.

*The planet Earth **travels** 66,620 miles around the sun.*

buy   drink   grow   increase   lay   make   post   produce
serve   spend

  a Volkswagen _____ 166 cars at Wolfsburg in West Germany.
  b The world _____ £75 million on all kinds of weapons.
  c Chickens at the Croton Farm, Ohio, USA _____ 154,166 eggs.
  d People in Britain _____ 1,426,940 letters.
  e McDonald's restaurants worldwide _____ 916,500 people.
  f The British _____ 156 tons of cat food for their 6.2 million cats.
  g The world _____ 12,540,000 Coca-Colas.
  h The Reynolds Tobacco Company, USA, _____ 13,640,872 cigarettes.
  i Your hair _____ 0.0018897 cms.
  j The world's population _____ by around 9,300.

2 Make a list of five things which you think happen every day in your country, town, or neighbourhood.

*Thousands of people **travel** to work by bus.*

Frequency adverbs ▶ 1.2

3 Use the list to make true statements, with *always, usually, often, sometimes, hardly ever, never*.

Copy my homework from another student.
*I **never** copy my homework from another student.*

  a Listen carefully to the teacher during the lesson.
  b Talk to the person sitting next to me.
  c Ask myself why on earth I am studying English!
  d Read English books or magazines, or listen to songs.
  e Look up all the new words in the coursebook before the lesson.
  f Try to answer the teacher's questions before the other students.
  g Look at other students' papers during tests.
  h Understand what I hear on the cassette player.
  i Read what I have written, and revise it carefully.
  j Ask someone if I don't understand something.

Past simple ▶ 2.1

4 This is part of an interview with a pop star about schooldays. Use the notes to make the questions the interviewer asked. Choose a verb from the list for the spaces. Put these verbs, and verbs given in brackets, into the correct form.

begin   buy   feel   fight   find   forget   leave   meet   spend
teach   write

You usually _____ to school on time? Or you (be) sometimes late?
Did you usually get to school on time? Or were you sometimes late?

a How old you (be) when you _____ school?
b You (think) that your teachers _____ you anything useful?
c Is it true that you _____ with other kids at school?
d How you _____ your free time after school?
e You _____ your school friends when you _____ school?
f How exactly you _____ when you _____ singing on TV?
g How you (start) writing songs? It (be) something you _____ easy to do?
h What about your first hit song, the one you _____ in a maths lesson?
i What (be) the first thing you _____ when you became rich?
j When you _____ your singing partner, Sandra, you (like) her?

5 Complete the singer's answers.

break   buy   drive   fall   give   hit   hurt   keep   know
leave   lose   sell   sing   think   understand

1 I _____ records in the market. And I _____ everyone crazy!
2 Not easy exactly, but I _____ I could do it well if I (try).
3 I (stay) until I was sixteen. In fact I _____ on my 16th birthday.
4 I _____ a calculator! No, actually I _____ my mum a car.
5 They _____ telling us everything was useful!
6 Yes. Actually, I wrote it during a test! I never _____ maths at school.
7 Yes, I was awful. Once I _____ a boy and _____ his nose.
8 Awful. I was so nervous I _____ over and _____ my arm.
9 I _____ she was nice-looking. And she _____ like Madonna, a bit.
10 I _____ touch with some of them. I (live) near most of them until last year.

6 Match the answers from 5 with the questions in 4.

SKILLS: LISTENING AND WRITING

Pre-listening

1 Do you have a good memory? What can you remember about your first school? Think of three happy memories, and one unhappy one!

Listening

2 Listen to three people talking about the schools they used to go to. Tick (✓) the topics each one talks about. The first tick has been put in for you. Were the speakers happy at school?

	uniform	teachers	homework	punishment	friends
Louise	✓				
Jim					
Debbie					

3 Listen to the cassette again. Decide whether these statements are **true** (t) or **false** (f).

a Louise lived at her school.
b Louise liked her uniform.
c Jim used to have lunch at school.
d Most of Jim's teachers were old.
e Debbie didn't like her school.
f Debbie used to go to a pub with one of her friends.

Pre-writing

4 The pictures show Helen when she was at school, and now that she is a student at university. Talk about what she did then, and what she does now. Use these points.

daily routine   clothes   likes/dislikes
study   free time

Writing

5 Write two paragraphs about Helen beginning like this:

> When Helen was at school, she was not a very good student.
> ....
> ....
> ....
> ....
>
> However, now that Helen is at university, her life is very different.
> ....
> ....
> ....
> ....

6 Make a list of things you used to do, and things you do now. Use ideas from the list in question 4. Tell other members of the class about these things, using your notes.

7 Write two paragraphs about yourself, using your ideas from question 6. You can make the facts imaginary if you prefer.

Check your grammar

Past simple and present simple

1 Write the question form and negative form for these verbs.

a He left. _____ _____

b You have one. _____ _____

c She knew. _____ _____

d He lives here. _____ _____

e You write a lot. _____ _____

f She studies hard. _____ _____

2 Study these uses of the Present simple. Choose the best description of the meaning.

a I get up every morning at half past seven.
  1 An unchanging state.   **2** A habitual activity.

b The sun rises in the east.
  1 An eternal truth.   **2** An unchanging state.

c I like chocolate.
  1 An unchanging state.   **2** A habitual activity.

Build your vocabulary

Nouns, verbs, adjectives and adverbs

1 a Check that you know what these words do: **noun**, **verb**, **adjective**, **adverb**. Which one:
  1 is used to describe a thing?
  2 is an action?
  3 is a thing?
  4 is used to describe an action?

b Make nouns from these verbs.

  produce   revise   calculate   punish   entertain

  _____   _____   _____   _____

Word field: clothes

2 Write the names of ten articles of clothing from this unit. Divide your list into sections.

clothes for men   clothes for women   clothes for both

Practise your pronunciation

Vowel sounds

1 📼 Which vowel sounds do you find difficult? Listen and repeat this list of some basic sounds. Circle the words in the list which have a difficult vowel sound for you.

sit /sɪt/	her /hɜː/
met /met/	play /pleɪ/
sat /sæt/	buy /baɪ/
cut /kʌt/	toy /tɔɪ/
lot /lɒt/	go /gəʊ/
put /pʊt/	now /naʊ/
be /biː/	dear /dɪə/
far /faː/	there /ðeə/
tore /tɔː/	poor /pɔː/
too /tuː/	

Sounds /ɪ/ (*give*) and /iː/ (*dream*)

2 Study the list and try to decide the vowel sound in each word.

give	steal	which
sleeve	feed	hill
teach	hid	greet
fit		

📼 Listen and repeat.

3 📼 Listen and circle the word you hear in each pair.

live / leave	bid / bead
rich / reach	sit / seat
fill / feel	

·9

Unit 2 Earning a living

Talking about jobs

1 Where do these people work, and what does each one do?

Which of the jobs do you like, and which do you dislike? Can you say why?

2 What other things might each person shown below say about the job?

It is a tiring job and I work very long hours.

It is a satisfying job because I can help other people.

I spend most of the day typing.

10

LANGUAGE ACTIVITIES

▶ Routines and requirements
▶ Qualifications and abilities
▶ Likes and dislikes
▶ Personal qualities

1 Do you have a job? Do you like it? Or do you know what kind of job you want to do? Learn more about yourself in this section. Read the text and make notes about what a tour guide does. Use the headings given.

TOUR GUIDE

I'm a student and I only work as a guide during the summer, taking small parties of foreign tourists around London. It's more or less the same routine every day in this job, but I don't find it boring. First I meet the group, check the names, and make sure that everyone is on the bus. Then I explain what we are going to see. It's all quite simple. I suppose it's a tiring job. Each tour lasts about three hours, and I do the same tour twice a day, at 9.00 and again at 2.00. Of course, I have to speak very clearly, and I also have to answer a lot of questions. And I sometimes have problems or emergencies: somebody gets lost, or leaves a camera behind. That's very common! And I have to sort it all out! But it's an enjoyable job and I meet lots of interesting people. And I now know a lot about London!

hours   routine   job requirements   problems   advantages

2 What do you think is involved in these jobs? Make some notes and talk about the job.

job	hours	routine	requirements	problems	advantages
taxi driver					
waiter/ waitress					
secretary					
farmer					
actor					

Describing job requirements   9.1

Have to

I **have to speak** very clearly.

3 What do think you are good at? Make a list of four points. Tell other people about yourself.

Describing ability   8.1

I'm **good at** deal**ing** with people.
I'm **not much good at** organis**ing** things.
I **can** type.
I **know how to** drive.
Know how to is used for a learned ability.

4 What do you like and dislike most about doing a job?

Do you like ...

getting up early
working outdoors
having a routine

working long hours
working with your hands
working on your own

Describing likes and dislikes   8.8

I enjoy **travelling**.
I like **talking** to people.
I don't mind **working** late.
(It is not a problem for me.)
I hate **typing**.
I can't stand **sitting** all day.

What do you think the people in question 2 like or dislike about their jobs?

I expect that taxi drivers like talking to people.
I don't think that waiters enjoy working late at night.

5 Complete the questionnaire by choosing the points which best describe you.

Choosing a Job – Your Personal Strengths	
You enjoy taking decisions, and like having responsibility.	Yes/No
You like meeting and dealing with people.	Yes/No
You like using your mind, and thinking about problems.	Yes/No
You want to work as part of a team.	Yes/No
You enjoy doing exactly the same job every day.	Yes/No
You don't mind moving away from your family and friends.	Yes/No
You want a job which you don't have to think about too much.	Yes/No
You are good at working on your own.	Yes/No
You have some special skills. (You know how to type, for example.)	Yes/No
You like working inside. (In an office, for example.)	Yes/No

Ask other people to explain their answers. Make notes under these headings:

abilities   likes and dislikes   other points

Role play

6

Student A
Choose a job from this unit for your partner. Use the notes you made in question 5. Describe the job and its routines.

Student B
Explain why you like or dislike this job, and why it is or is not suitable for you. Describe a job that you like.

SKILLS: READING AND LISTENING

Pre-reading

1 Read this list of job features. Which do you think are most important?

working regular hours
meeting interesting people
travelling as part of the job
working long hours

being part of a large company
working for yourself
doing the same things every day
earning a high salary

Reading

2 The article below is about a make-up artist's working day. Before you read it, decide which job features in question 1 it will mention.

Read and find out if your predictions were correct.

Comprehension check

3 a Did Heidi always want to be a make-up artist?

b Is her daily routine always the same? What was her job on this day?

c How many people did she make up in the job she describes? Did anyone help her?

d What does she do at the end of the day? What else did she do after this job?

One Make-Up Artist's Day

1 Heidi Miller is 22 and has been a make-up artist since she was 16. She's worked for most magazines, including *Vogue*, toured the world
5 with groups, and made up <u>dozens of</u> famous faces.

'I became a make-up artist by accident,' she explains. 'I got in touch with a photographer I knew and
10 went to work as his assistant. Then one day the make-up artist he'd booked didn't <u>turn up</u>, so I did it instead. It was easy and I enjoyed it, so a few months later I left and
15 <u>assisted</u> a few well-known make-up artists to learn the skills.

'I suppose it sounds like a glamorous and well-paid job, but it isn't,' she <u>points out</u>. 'Sometimes you may
20 only get one booking a week and it can be months until the client pays you for it. On the good side, you may get to travel. Because you never know when you're going to be work-
25 ing, though, it's hard to book holidays or organise a social life, so you've got to be dedicated.'

9.00. Today I had a job at *Riva* magazine so I had to be at the photogra-
30 pher's studio at 9.30. Had to struggle in on the Underground with all my bags.

10.00. <u>Had a chat</u> to the features editor of the magazine about the sort of
35 look they wanted. The feature was about four very glamorous mums and their daughters, so there were eight people to make up. Sometimes I have to do all the hair as well, but
40 this time there was a hairdresser. When I'm doing real people (not models or famous people) I try to chat to them about what I'm doing and how they like to look. Between
45 us we managed to get two people ready in an hour, then I had to stand by as the photographer took the pictures in case we needed more powder to stop a shiny nose or
50 something. First of all the photographer takes a Polaroid picture and I check to see that the person doesn't have bags under their eyes or un-even lipstick, or something that only
55 shows up under the strong lights. Lips are the <u>trickiest</u> to do; nearly everyone has uneven lips and you need a steady hand to balance them up.

60 12.30. Stopped for lunch. The photographer or magazine you're working for usually sends out for sandwiches. Lunch gives you a good chance to gossip, but afterwards you
65 have to go round doing everyone's lips again.

1.15. Back to work. This was an easy job because the photos were portraits and the 'models' just had bits of
70 velvet over their shoulders. When there are proper outfits you have to consider the styles and colours, but this time they just left it up to me, which is much nicer.

75 5.00 Phoned my agent to see where I'd be working the next day. This time I didn't have a booking so I had a free day to look forward to. I like working with bands best because
80 you can be really cheeky to them and it's a good laugh, but there's nothing I hate doing, really.

6.00. Finished the shoot. Often in the evenings you go back to the pho-
85 tographer's where you worked a few days earlier to see how the <u>shots</u> turned out and maybe get a few for your book, but this time I just packed up and went to see my boyfriend.
90 But every night you have to sterilise all the brushes and sponges used during the day and tidy out your <u>kit</u>. It makes your living, so you've got to look after it!

Word search

4 Put words or phrases from this list in place of the words underlined in the text.

most difficult to do	photographs
arrive	helped
lots of	equipment
explains	had a talk

Speaking

5 Find two things you like, and two things you don't like, about Heidi's job.

6 What kind of person do you think you have to be to succeed as a make-up artist? Choose from the list and explain. Can you add any other ideas?

versatile
You have to be versatile, because the job changes from day to day.

You have to be:	**You have to have:**	**You have to be good at:**
versatile	interest in the job	foreign languages
reliable	qualifications	selling things
hardworking	stamina	getting on with people

Describe some other jobs in the same way.

You have to be versatile to be a police officer, because the job is never the same.
You need a lot of stamina to be an air stewardess. Looking after the passengers during a long flight can be very tiring.

Listening

7 ▭ Listen to part of a radio programme about job interviews. Tick (✓) the items in question 6 which are mentioned.

8 ▭ Read this list of sentences. Listen again, and decide whether the speaker said the words given here, or not.

a *I work with the financial director.*
b *What kind of people do you want?*
c *We expect all our employees to be truthful . . .*
d *Do you expect everyone to have the same qualities?*
e *Some people don't like to be part of a team . . .*
f *It depends what kind of job you want.*

9 Think of five questions to ask someone in a job interview.

14

Obligation: describing rules ▶ 9

1 Study this list of rules which has just been given to you by your new boss. Restate the rules using *have to*, or *(not) be allowed to*. You can change the formal language of the rules and use informal language.

No cars are to be parked in the car park without permission.
***I'm not allowed to park my car** in the car park without permission.*

a All staff are required to be punctual and to be in the office by 9.00.
b This is a no-smoking office. Smoking is only permitted in the smokers' rest room, and only during tea breaks and lunch breaks.
c Staff are expected to wear suitable clothes i.e. not jeans, etc.
d Staff are not to use the telephone to make personal calls. Personal calls received by staff should be kept to a minimum.
e All staff work one Saturday morning each month, to be arranged with the office supervisor.
f No personal possessions (e.g. plants, photographs, etc.) should be placed on desks in view of the public.
g Staff dealing with members of the public are required to be polite and helpful at all times.
h The management cannot pay any part of the monthly salary before the usual date, or lend money in any way.

2 Decide whether each statement means:
A It is the rule, to do this, or not do this.
B It is my personal opinion, or a rule made by me.
C This is not necessary.

You must start putting more effort into your work. **B**

a You have to take all the letters to the Post Office by 12.30.
b You don't have to work late if you don't want to.
c You aren't allowed to use these stamps for your personal letters.
d You really mustn't be so rude to people on the phone.
e You can't make long-distance calls just to talk with your friends.
f You don't have to come in tomorrow, I think I can manage.
g You must be a bit more careful when you deal with money.
h You have to keep this form and give it to your next employer.
i You're allowed to smoke if the others in the office agree.
j You don't have to wear a tie, you know.

Present and past

3 Complete each sentence **a** to **f** with a suitable ending from **1** to **6**.

  a I took a job as a shop assistant ...
  b I usually stop work between 12.30. and 1.30. ...
  c I used to take the bus to work ...
  d I used to work as a journalist on the local paper ...
  e I always get on well with my boss ...
  f I left my job at the Post Office ...

  1 ... but now I drive because it's a lot quicker.
  2 ... but she doesn't always treat me very kindly.
  3 ... but I decided to leave after only two weeks.
  4 ... and I work in a bank now.
  5 ... but it wasn't very interesting.
  6 ... and I go for a snack in the local pub.

4 Make five statements about your own job, an imaginary job, or about school if you prefer. Say what you *like, enjoy* or *can't stand doing*.

  *I like meeting people, but I **can't stand sitting** in an office all day.*

Present simple or present continuous ▶ 1.1, 1.3, 1.5

5 Put the verbs in brackets into either present simple or present continuous in each sentence.

  a Mr Young (talk) on the phone at the moment. Could you phone back later?
  b I (work) in the Accounts Department just for this week.
  c I (write) a lot of letters in this job.
  d Why (everyone/leave)? What (happen)?
  e My boss (leave) early every Friday, so we (not work) very hard on Friday afternoons.
  f I (like) my new job, but the other people in the office (not talk) to me very much.
  g Can you talk to this customer, please? The phone (ring) and I have to answer it.
  h Mr Smith, a customer (wait) for you!

Requests and orders
▶ 8.10, 8.14

6 Decide which are **requests**, and which are **orders**.

  a Do you think you could make me some coffee?
  b Bring those letters, will you?
  c Could you type these letters again please?
  d Take these files to Room 101.
  e Do you think you could possibly lend me a hand?
  f Phone the Accounts Department, can you?
  g Do you think you could turn on the air conditioning?
  h Could you leave the report on my desk?

7 Practise making requests to other members of the class.

Pre-writing

1 Complete this text, using the words and phrases given.

1 [1] _____ journalist on a local newspaper. [2] _____ my job, and [3] _____ most of the time. [4] _____ I meet some interesting people, and I don't stay in the office all the time.
2 [5] _____, there are several disadvantages. [6] _____ the job is [7] _____ because I am a trainee. [8] _____ some of the things I have to do are rather [9] _____.
3 I do the same kinds of things every day [10] _____ .

[11] _____ I have a meeting with my editor, who decides which stories are important. [12] _____ I go out to interview people, and take notes for my story. [13] _____ I use a cassette recorder. [14] _____ write the stories so that they are ready by Thursday at 5.00pm. My editor often tells me to make the story shorter or change it. [15] _____ is when I read my work in the newspaper.

first of all
sometimes
the good side of this job is that
but there is a lot of variety in my work
I work as a
boring
I enjoy

I have to
not very well-paid
it is interesting
every day
on the other hand
another problem is that
the best part of my job
then

2 Choose a title for paragraphs **1**, **2** and **3** in question 1.

My ambitions for the future.
The routine in my job.
The disadvantages of the job.

My job and its advantages.
The reason I took my job.
How to become a journalist.

Pre-listening

3 Use these pictures to describe what a bank cashier does. Base your description on the text in question 1.

Listening

4 🔲 Listen to a bank cashier describing her job. <u>Underline</u> the parts of each statement which are correct.

She works as the manager of a large bank in the city centre.

a It's not a very interesting job, and she wants to leave.
b She might go to another department in a different bank.
c She has to check the money in the till and put it in the nightsafe.
d Some customers get impatient because she does her work quickly.
e She has to be careful because she mustn't drop the money.
f The job is badly paid but has good prospects for the future.
g Although it is a routine job, it can be exciting sometimes.

Writing

5 Write a description of a bank cashier's job based on question 3. Begin:

Janet works as a cashier in a large bank in the city centre ...

6 Write a similar text about your own job, or an imaginary job. Begin:

I work as a ...

STUDY FOCUS

Check your grammar

Present simple and present continuous

1 a Choose the best explanation for each sentence.

I type my letters.   **1** Always   **2** At the moment.
I'm typing letters.   **1** Always   **2** At the moment.

b Study these examples and decide why the verbs used are usually in simple forms only. Can we explain the meaning by using *always* or *at the moment* as we could in **a**?

I want a job which involves travelling.
I know what he means, because I understand Russian.

Rules and obligation

2 How could you answer each question? Choose from the answers given.

a Can I use a dictionary during the exam?
Sorry, you mustn't.
Sorry, you don't have to.
Sorry, you are not allowed to.

b Can you work late tonight?
Yes, I mustn't be home until 7.00
Yes, I don't have to be home until 7.00.

c How does this phone work?
You must press both of these switches.
You have to press both of these switches.

Build your vocabulary

Word search

1 Find words which fit the definitions. These words have appeared in Unit 2.

a not polite	r	_____
b talk informally	c	_____
c allowed	p	_____
d a person who works for a wage	e	_____
e person who works in a garage	m	_____
f person who runs a newspaper	e	_____

Word field: jobs

2 Make a list of all the jobs, and words connected with finding jobs and working, in Unit 2.

Practise your pronunciation

Past tense -*ed* endings

1 a 🔊 Listen and repeat the past tense forms in the list.

forced	hated
asked	washed
decided	allowed
helped	worked
liked	watched
stayed	cleaned

b Complete this rule for pronouncing -*ed* endings.

1 If the sound -*ed* is /t/ or /d/, -*ed* is pronounced

_____ .

2 If the sound is /k/, /p/, /s/, /ʃ/ or /tʃ/, -*ed* is pronounced

_____ .

3 For other sounds before -*ed*, -*ed* is pronounced

_____ .

2 🔊 Decide how to pronounce this list of past tense forms. Listen and check your pronunciation.

waited	looked
stared	lined
hunted	missed
masked	headed
punched	sighted

Unit 3   It couldn't happen to me

STARTING POINTS

What happened?

1 Use the pictures to plan a story. Use your own ideas for the blank picture.

2 Tell your version of the story to other members of the class.

Begin like this:

EYEWITNESS REPORT

NAME: _____

I was on my way to my English lesson, and I saw exactly what happened...

LANGUAGE ACTIVITIES

▶ Narrative contrasts
▶ Past simple and past continuous

1 Read the endings of three stories. Try to guess what happened in each one.

a *He said, 'I'm sorry I was so long, but the bus for Manchester was parked at the back.'*
b *We found the bus in the end, but we didn't see very much of the old town!*
c *But when I tried to talk to him, he disappeared in a flash of light.*

2 The pictures on the right show the main parts of one of the stories in question 1.

Tell the story. Is your story the same as everyone else's? Write down the verbs you used.

3 Read these extracts from another story in question 1. Can you guess what happened?

We asked for directions from passers-by, but nobody could understand us.

Then we met an old man and he started talking to us.

He thought we wanted a hotel and he took us to one near the market.

Last year we decided to go to North Africa for a holiday.

One day we went on a guided tour to the old part of the town.

We decided to go back to the bus, but we couldn't find it.

These pictures show other parts of the story. What do they show? Add this information to the story and tell the story from the beginning.

1

2

3

Past simple

For a list of irregular verbs see **21**

Past continuous and past simple 2.2, 2.1

*While we **were walking** through the market, we **saw** some souvenirs.*

1   2   3

4 Tell a story about something which happened to you. Use one or more of these ideas.

5 Read the newspaper extract. Do you believe that it's true?

I MET
ELVIS
TEN YEARS AFTER HIS DEATH

1 If you thought that the King was dead, but his music lived on, then you are wrong, according to a waitress from Kettering. Because
5 Elvis is still alive – and 36-year-old Angela Dutton, saw him in Northampton in 1987. 'I was going home on the bus late one night. He was dressed as a bus conductor, I
10 recognised him immediately,' she told our reporter. 'I know that people will say that I am crazy, but it was him. When I paid my fare on the bus, I looked into his eyes and I
15 could see the suffering of all those years.' But why should Elvis suddenly show up in Britain, a country he never visited while he was alive? 'He knows his greatest
20 fans are here,' Angela told me.

The reporter who interviewed Angela asked the questions given below. What were Angela's answers?

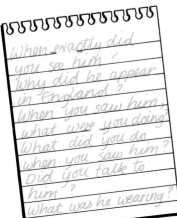

6 What other questions would you ask Angela? What questions did the reporter ask to get the information below?

'I looked for him several times after that, but I never saw him again.'

'Nothing at all, he just stared. I couldn't say anything either.'

'I don't think so. I'm sure I was the only one who saw him.'

'He was just standing there, waiting for me to ask for my ticket.'

'It was like being in a dream. When I got home I still felt as if I was floating.'

Role play

7 Read the headlines. What happened in the stories?

Student A
Last week you had a very strange experience. Tell your story to a reporter.

Student B
You are a reporter. Ask questions to find out exactly what happened. Make some notes of the answers.

SKILLS: READING AND LISTENING

Pre-reading

1 Read the headlines and decide what happened in each story.

a BIRMINGHAM FAMILY FIRST HOME IN PACIFIC RACE

d BRITISH BOAT FAMILY SAFE AFTER THREE DAYS

b TRAGEDY AT SEA – Three Missing

c FAMILY RESCUED FROM SPANISH HIJACK

e TOURISTS ARRESTED AFTER STEALING YACHT

Reading

2 Read the newspaper story and decide which headline from question 1 goes with it. Guess which words are missing from the text.

1   A British family, Mr Raymond Kearne, his wife Jacqueline and their son James, aged seven, have survived a three-day ordeal at sea with no food or [1] _____ after a holiday boat trip in Majorca turned into a nightmare.

2   Mr Kearne, aged 48, and his family, from Birmingham, were stranded off the coast of the Balearic island of Dragonera after their ten-foot motor launch ran out of [2] _____ . They were rescued on Monday, suffering from sunburn, exhaustion, starvation and dehydration.

3   They were staying in a private villa in the resort of Santa Ponsa and on Saturday decided to make a short trip around the coast to a nearby [3] _____ . They took no extra provisions or fuel. Mr Kearne returned to the shore when he realised he was running low on fuel. But he was unable to land because of rocks and was forced to steer out. When his fuel ran out entirely, strong winds and an undercurrent took the boat 20 miles out to sea.

4   'I tried rowing but it was useless,' said Mr Kearne. 'I tried to keep calm. We all thought that a [4] _____ would find us and help us. Many fishing boats passed and we waved and yelled, but nobody saw us. At night it was terrifying – black and stormy. The waves got bigger and bigger. It was hell. Several large cruisers and ferry boats passed and my wife and I feared one of them might run us down.'

5   Mr Kearne tried to rig up a sail as an awning to protect them against the sun but it was torn away by the [5] _____ . A fisherman finally raised the alarm when he saw them waving frantically. Mr Kearne said that he thought that if they had not been rescued, he and his wife might have lasted two more days, and his son perhaps only one.

3 Each sentence below gives one of the main points of the story. Find the paragraph of the text which contains each point.

  a The weather was bad during the night, and they thought a ship would hit them.
  b The wind and the sea carried the boat far away from the shore.
  c It was difficult to protect themselves from the sun, and they tried to use a sail to make a shelter.
  d They waved at boats but nobody noticed them.
  e They were finally rescued because they waved a lot at a fishing boat.
  f They were not in a good condition after three days.
  g They did not have any extra food or petrol.

Word search

4 Find words in the text which could be replaced by:

difficult or painful experience
bad dream
extreme tiredness
holiday town
completely
shouted

5 Make a list of five questions to ask the Kearne family about their experience as described in question 2. Ask a partner to find the answers in the text.

Pre-listening

6 Study the three pictures. Write a short news story for each one.

Listening

7 ▭ Listen to three radio news stories. How different are the stories you wrote?

8 ▭ Listen to the stories again and decide if these statements are **true** (t) or **false** (f).

a Some dolphins attacked Brian Rafferty's surfboard.
b Brian Rafferty is not the first person saved in this way.
c The train crashed on a busy main road.
d The driver tried to catch the train by running after it.
e Mary's flowers were not supposed to grow.
f Another person checked that the flowers were growing.

GRAMMAR PRACTICE

Past simple and past continuous ▶ 2.1, 2.2

1 Study the pictures and decide what happened to these three people.

2 Complete each sentence **a** to **h** with a suitable ending from **1** to **8**. Which people are the sentences about? Do the sentences explain what happened in the pictures? Tell your version of the story.

  a When Jan came home from jogging, ...
  b Her flatmate Sue was not at home...
  c While Jan was getting the ladder from the garden, ...
  d When Jan started climbing the ladder, ...
  e Mrs Lee thought that Jan was a burglar...
  f When Jan reached the top of the ladder, ...
  g While Sue was having a shower, ...
  h When Jan heard the scream, ...

  1 ... she tried to open the window.
  2 ... she was frightened and fell off the ladder.
  3 ... so she called the police.
  4 ... she realised that she didn't have her keys.
  5 ... she saw Jan's face at the window and screamed.
  6 ... Mrs Lee, who lived opposite, saw her.
  7 ... so Jan decided to climb in through the bathroom window.
  8 ... Sue came home unexpectedly.

Past simple and past continuous: asking questions
▶ 2.1, 2.2

3 These are the answers to some questions which the police asked the three people in the pictures. Decide what the questions were. Use the question words given.

I saw someone trying to break into the house. (WHO)
Who did you see in the garden?

  a I didn't have my keys with me and I thought that Sue was out. (WHY)
  b I was trying to get in through the bathroom window. (WHY)
  c I was having a shower, actually. It was rather frightening. (WHAT)
  d I screamed, I'm afraid, and then I ran into the kitchen. (WHAT)
  e I saw her carrying the ladder and thought she was a burglar. (WHY)

1 JAN

2 MRS LEE

3 SUE

Prepositions of place and movement ▶ 18

4 Read this continuation of the story. Put a suitable preposition into each space. Choose from:

at   in   into   on   out   to

The policeman got [1] _____ the patrol car and drove away, and the girl went [2] _____ Mrs Lee's house for some tea. When they went [3] _____ the kitchen, Mrs Lee couldn't find her purse which she thought was [4] _____ the table. She thought a burglar had stolen it! Sue went [5] _____ to see if there was anyone [6] _____ the garden. Then she noticed a man sitting [7] _____ the pavement [8] _____ the end of the street. But just then a bus stopped [9] _____ the bus stop and the man got [10] _____. So she called the police.

Past simple and past continuous: which tense? ▶ 2.1, 2.2

5 This text completes the description of what happened. Put each verb in brackets into the most suitable past tense.

When the police [1 arrive] for the second time, they [2 ask] a lot more questions. They [3 not seem] to believe the story about Mrs Lee's handbag. They [4 search] the house, and then, while they [5 have] a cup of tea in the kitchen, they [6 question] Sue about the man she had seen. 'He [7 wear] a raincoat, and I think he [8 smoke] a pipe,' she [9 tell] them. Then the police [10 become] more interested in the story, because, by coincidence, they [11 look] for a burglar of this description. However, just then Mrs Lee [12 find] her purse in her coat pocket.

6 Complete the text by using each verb in the correct tense once only.

call   carry   climb
come back   decide
fall off   go out   happen
look out   realise   take
think   try   wait   not want

This is a summary of the silly story of Jan, Sue and the ladder.

One morning Jan [1] _____ jogging. When she [2] _____, she [3] _____ that her flatmate, Sue, was not in, and she [4] _____ to wait outside in the cold. So Jan [5] _____ to borrow a ladder from her neighbour, Mrs Lee. She [6] _____ the ladder from Mrs Lee's garden and [7] _____ it back to the house. While Jan [8] _____ up the ladder and [9] _____ to get in upstairs, Mrs Lee [10] _____ of her kitchen window and [11] _____ Jan was a burglar. So Mrs Lee [12] _____ the police, but while she [13] _____ for them to arrive, something strange [14] _____ . The 'burglar' suddenly [15] _____ the ladder, and Mrs Lee realised that he looked a lot like Jan.

Listening

1 📼 Listen to this telephone call between Roger and his friend Ann. Complete the directions Ann gives Roger, and the instructions for what he has to do. Each space is ONE word.

Turn off the motorway to South Longwell. Follow the road to [1] _____ [2] _____ . Then turn [3] _____ . After the park, turn [4] _____ at the [5] _____ [6] _____ and take the road to Leicester. 'Kingston Court' is on the [7] _____ , five minutes down the road, after a [8] _____ , Mr Stubbs's office is on the [9] _____ floor. Give him the [10] _____ and then bring the [11] _____ back here.

2 📼 Look at the map which Roger drew. Is it correct? Listen to the cassette again if necessary. Do you think that Roger found 'Kingston Court' easily?

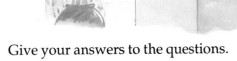

Pre-writing

3 Study the picture and decide what happened:

before Roger arrived at 'Kingston Court'
when he got there
after that

Give your answers to the questions.

a What did Ann ask Roger to do?
b What happened when he followed his map?
c Why were the police in Mr Stubbs's office?
d What was in the parcel?
e What happened in the end?

Writing

4 Plan the story of Roger's day. Discuss your plan.

Write your story and show it to others.

5 Plan a story about something that happened to you on holiday. Use these phrases as a guide.

While I was on holiday . . .
Unfortunately I didn't have . . .
I decided to go to . . .
When I got there I found that . . .
Then I had a good idea . . .
I decided to spend the day . . .
While I was waiting . . .
I lost my way and so . . .
In the end I . . .
I managed to . . .

STUDY FOCUS

Check your grammar

Narrative tenses

1 Read the extract below and complete the table, using verbs from the extract.

When I sat down in the train compartment, I started to read Mrs Henderson's letter. The three other people were either gazing out of the window or reading newspapers, and I didn't pay much attention to them. I was still trying to understand exactly what her strange message meant, when we stopped at a station. My companions left the train, and a tall bearded man entered the compartment. He sat opposite me, and stared at me. I remembered Mrs Henderson's description of her attacker, and reached for my revolver. 'Relax, Watson,' said the stranger. 'That will not be necessary.' 'Good heavens, Holmes, what on earth are you doing dressed like that?' I stuttered...

main narrative events	background description
sat down started	were gazing

2 Do you have a similar contrast in your own language?

Build your vocabulary

Words often confused

1 Use your dictionary to make sure you understand the difference between the words in each pair. Write sentences for each pair to make the difference in meaning clear.

a miss/lose ....
....

b frightening/frightened ....
....

c dress/wear (verbs) ....
....

d tired/exhausted ....
....

e look at/look for ....
....

Practise your pronunciation

Consonant sounds

1 Each pair of words contains an important difference in consonant sounds. Can you tell the difference between the sounds underlined?

pill/bill   fine/pine
tie/die   this/thick
dog/dock   thin/tin
run/rung   then/den
view/few   seat/sheet
van/ban   ice/eyes

🎧 Listen and repeat each pair. Which pairs are difficult for you?

Word stress

2 Study the words below from this unit. Decide which part of the word is stressed most. <u>Underline</u> the most heavily stressed syllable.

coincidence
necessary
frightening
attention
realise
interested
opposite
reporter

🎧 Listen and repeat.

When you learn a new word, make sure you learn which syllable has most stress

matches
6 lamb chops
½ kilo cheese
aspirins
newspaper
cabbage
film

Unit 4 It's a bargain

STARTING POINTS

Shops and shopping

1 Where can you buy the things on the shopping list?

Name four other kinds of shop. What can you buy in each one?

Do you do a lot of shopping? Make lists of things you buy from shops. Compare lists.

every day   every week   when necessary   very rarely

2 What do you think the customer and shop assistant in the picture are saying?

Read what the customers say and suggest possible replies.

customer

How much is this cheese?
What's good for insect bites?
I want to send this express.
Have you got any tomatoes?

Which of these is the best?
Are they fresh?
How much does that weigh?

Match the replies with these questions.

shop assistant

I've read this one and it's good.
Yes, still warm.
It's just over 2 kilos.
It's £4.25 a kilo.

The other counter, please.
Sorry, we've just run out.
This cream is about the best.

LANGUAGE ACTIVITIES

▶ Choosing presents
▶ Going shopping

1 Use the questionnaire to ask and answer questions about shopping habits.

HOW DO YOU SHOP?

1 When you go into a shop: **a** you usually know exactly what you want. **b** you only want to look. **c** you always look carefully and come back later to buy.	**2** You prefer to go shopping: **a** in small local shops where you know people. **b** large stores in the city centre. **c** anywhere which is cheap.	**3** You mainly go shopping for: **a** food or drink. **b** clothes or shoes. **c** records or books.
4 You usually go shopping: **a** alone. **b** with family. **c** with friends.	**5** You think first about: **a** the price. **b** the quality. **c** the name.	**6** You take advice from: **a** shop assistants. **b** friends or family. **c** nobody.

Compare answers and decide which description fits you best.

Fun Shopper You enjoy it! And it's more interesting for you if you go with a friend!	***Practical Shopper*** You get the best and the cheapest!	***Reluctant Shopper*** You hate doing it! You're happier when someone tells you what to buy!

2 Choose a present for a friend or relative from the presents shown. Say who the person is, what you are going to buy, and why.

£30.00
£12.00
£6.50
£40.00
£7.95
£7.50
£20.00

> **Describing plans**
>
> **Going to 4.2**
>
> I'm **going to buy** my brother a calculator.

> **Making comparisons with adjectives 14.2**
>
> An iron is **more useful than** a coffee maker.
> Oh, I don't think so.
> I think that something personal is **better**.

Do you think that the presents shown are good ones? Think of some more suitable presents, and explain why they are better.

3 Study the pictures and decide what the people are saying.

Will and shall   4.1

Decision of the moment
I'll wear it now.

Making a promise
I'll be back in a minute.

Making an offer
Shall I carry it?
I'll help you.

☎ Listen to the mini-dialogues which go with the pictures. Decide which dialogue goes with each picture.

Note down what people in the dialogue say when they make a **promise**, an **offer**, a **decision of the moment** and a **suggestion**.

Look at the pictures and act out the situations in your own words.

Making a suggestion   8.15

How about buying her a ring?
What about a blue one?

4 What problems do these people have with the clothes they are trying on? Match what they say with the pictures.

The sleeves are too short, I think.   *They're not tight enough.*
It's too large.   *It's not big enough.*
They're not wide enough.   *It's much too long.*

Too and not enough   13.2

This jacket is too tight.
The trousers are not long enough.

Role play

5

Student A	Student B
You want to buy some clothes but you can't decide what to buy. Ask the assistant for help, try on the clothes. Explain why you don't want them.	You are the shop assistant. Serve the customer and suggest what to buy. Discuss prices, sizes and colours. Try to persuade the customer to buy something, and make a sale.

Reading

1 Describe the products shown, and say what you think they are for.

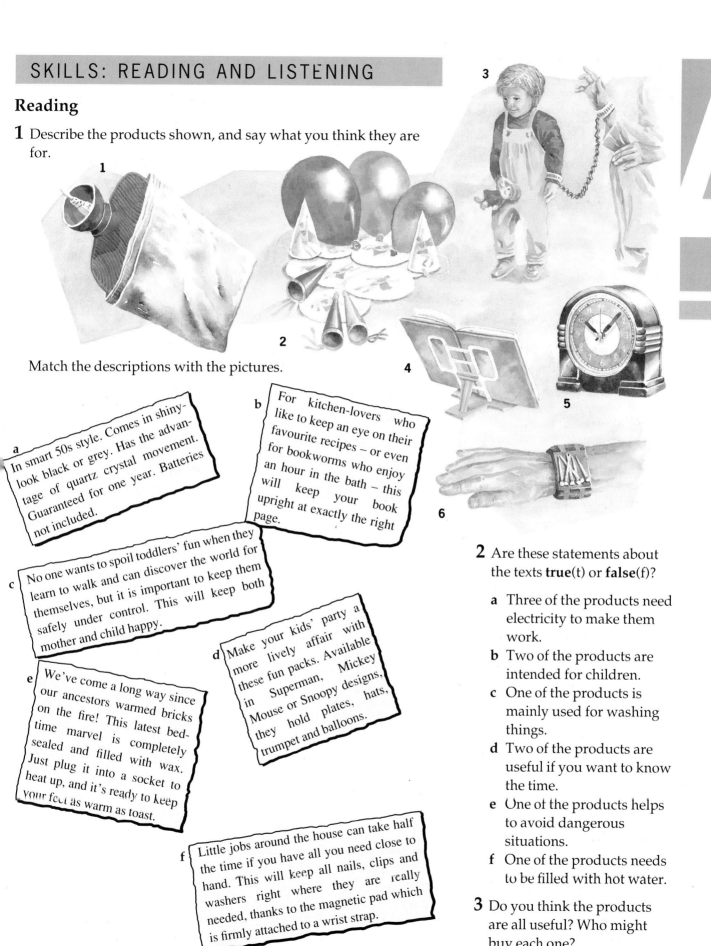

Match the descriptions with the pictures.

a In smart 50s style. Comes in shiny-look black or grey. Has the advantage of quartz crystal movement. Guaranteed for one year. Batteries not included.

b For kitchen-lovers who like to keep an eye on their favourite recipes – or even for bookworms who enjoy an hour in the bath – this will keep your book upright at exactly the right page.

c No one wants to spoil toddlers' fun when they learn to walk and can discover the world for themselves, but it is important to keep them safely under control. This will keep both mother and child happy.

d Make your kids' party a more lively affair with these fun packs. Available in Superman, Mickey Mouse or Snoopy designs, they hold plates, hats, trumpet and balloons.

e We've come a long way since our ancestors warmed bricks on the fire! This latest bed-time marvel is completely sealed and filled with wax. Just plug it into a socket to heat up, and it's ready to keep your feet as warm as toast.

f Little jobs around the house can take half the time if you have all you need close to hand. This will keep all nails, clips and washers right where they are really needed, thanks to the magnetic pad which is firmly attached to a wrist strap.

2 Are these statements about the texts **true**(t) or **false**(f)?

a Three of the products need electricity to make them work.

b Two of the products are intended for children.

c One of the products is mainly used for washing things.

d Two of the products are useful if you want to know the time.

e One of the products helps to avoid dangerous situations.

f One of the products needs to be filled with hot water.

3 Do you think the products are all useful? Who might buy each one?

31

Reading

4 Do people buy products by post in your country? What might go wrong when you buy things in this way?

Read these comments made by customers. Which ones refer to products shown in question 1?

a *When I tried on the product I had ordered, it was definitely not the size I had asked for in my order. Also the style was different, as I asked for one to match the ear-rings I had ordered. I am returning the one you sent me and would like to repeat my original order.*

b *I'm afraid that I find your advertisement very misleading. I have tried your product with several different kinds of books, and in each case the whole thing fell over. In the end it fell to pieces.*

c *I bought one of these products recently and I would like to point out that it is not at all safe. My young daughter was nearly burnt recently when she managed to undo the top, and the contents spilled all over the floor. I feel strongly that you should make it clear that this product is not completely childproof.*

d *I received my order for your product last week and have only just found that it does not contain the things listed in your advertisement. The magnetic pad and the batteries were missing. I would be grateful if you could send these to me by return of post.*

Pre-listening

5 Have you ever received a free gift with a product? Do offers of free gifts make you buy products?

Listening

6 📼 Listen to a conversation about free gifts. Match the products listed below with the free gifts which were given.

gifts		products	
bucket	plastic animal	breakfast cereal	shampoo
comb	picture cards	petrol	washing powder
glasses	jigsaw puzzle	ice-cream	chewing gum

Speaking

7 What else makes you decide to buy something?

a cut-price offer
seeing a new product
an advertisement
the wrapping or packaging

8 Re-arrange the lines of this advertisement, so that they are in a suitable order.

a It acts fast too.
b But when you have one, then you need the best solution around.
c Splitting headache?
d When the going gets rough, full-strength Nopain 500 helps you find your feet.
e Full strength Nopain, for instance.
f So it'll deal with your headache in no time.
g In today's busy world, a headache is the last thing you need.
h Each tablet contains 500mg of paracetamol, a pain-killer doctors recommend.
i Nopain 500 will ease your pain.
j And it won't harm your stomach.

Which words need capitals? Suggest a picture to go with the advertisement.

9 Describe your favourite advertisement. Write your own advertisement for a new imaginary product.

GRAMMAR PRACTICE

Present continuous: present use and future use
▶ 1.3, 4.4

1 Read the sentences below, and write **now** or **future** beside each one, according to the situation.

*You can't talk to Jim, **he's taking** a bath.* **(now)**
***I'm meeting** Katie outside the shop.* **(future)**

a I'm getting some more cassettes for my birthday.
b I'm paying for the stereo when I collect it.
c I'm looking for a green pullover. Can you help me?
d The price is going up soon, I'm afraid.
e Look! They're selling everything at half price!
f They're having a sale on Saturday.
g Jack's taking us out to lunch afterwards.
h The manager's talking on the phone, I'm afraid.

Future use of present continuous and *going to*
▶ 4.4, 4.2

2 Use the words given to complete each sentence. Use present continuous for a **fixed arrangement**, and *going to* for a **plan**.

Would you like to come round on Saturday? We/have/party.
Would you like to come round on Saturday?
We are having a party **fixed arrangement**

I'm not sure, but I think I/buy/a computer.
I'm not sure, but I think I'm going to buy a computer **plan**

a This summer before we go camping I/buy/new tent.
b What/you/do on Thursday morning? Would you like to come shopping?
c I've got my plane ticket for Canada. I/leave on the 15th.
d The car won't start! What/we/do now? We could walk, I suppose.
e I can't stand this flat. I think I/move to a new area.
f See you tomorrow. We/meet outside the station at 12.00.
g Sorry I can't see you tomorrow. I/fly to Paris in the morning.
h When I have the money I/buy a new carpet for the living room.
i Do you remember that Dutch friend of ours? She/come to stay with us in the summer.
j I don't like the colour of the shirt I bought. I/take it back to the shop.

Uses of *will* ▶ 4.1

3 Match the sentences with the words which best explain each sentence.

I'll take this one.
decision of the moment
Shall I do it for you?
making an offer
I'll meet you at the bus stop.
making an arrangement
I'll be there, don't worry.
making a promise

a Shall I carry that bag for you?
b I'll see you outside the shop.
c Thank you, but I think I'll wait, if that's all right.
d I'll come back for the other books on Friday, if that's all right.
e I'll pay you the money I owe you next weekend.
f I like these, but I'll take the large pair
g You've got a lot of things, shall I put them all in the bag?
h I won't drop the eggs, don't worry.

4 Make sentences according to the instructions, using the language practised in question 3.

Decide to take the blue one.
I'll take the blue one.

a Arrange to meet your friend outside the chemist's at 6.30.
b Offer to buy a hamburger for your friend.
c Promise to pay back the money you owe your friend on Friday.
d Decide to take the first pair of shoes you tried on.
e Offer to write your name and address on the back of the cheque.
f Decide to buy your father the yellow shirt with the pink stripes.

Making comparisons with adjectives ▶ 14

5 Compare the ways of shopping, using the words given in brackets. Add explanations where possible.

*Using local shops is **more convenient than** going to the centre.*
*Large shops are **cheaper than** small local shops. This is because they sell more things, so they can reduce prices.*

a supermarkets/small grocers   (cheap)
b expensive clothes/cheap clothes   (good quality)
c department stores/small shops   (interesting)
d staff in small shops/staff in supermarkets   (happy)
e street markets/ordinary shops   (economical)
f local 'corner' shops/other shops   (expensive)
g buying by post/going to shops   (difficult)
h products in advertisements/the real thing   (good)

Comparatives and superlatives ▶ 14.1, 14.2, 14.3

6 Complete each sentence and give your own opinion.

*People say that Tokyo is **the most expensive** city in the world.*

*Some people say that London is **more interesting than** Paris.*

a Generally speaking, gold jewellery is more . . .
b Finding exactly what you want to buy is the most . . .
c When they go shopping, teenagers are not as . . .
d Going shopping with your family is more . . .
e Buying presents for others is not as . . .
f Looking around the shops on Saturday morning is the most . . .
g Going to the supermarket is worse . . .
h Paying with a credit card is not as . . .

Too and *very* ▶ 13.2

7 Comment on each suggestion, using *too* or *very*.

Why don't you buy your little brother a skateboard?
*He's **too** young for something like that. Skateboards are **very** dangerous.*

a Why don't you buy your sister an electric mixer?
b How about giving your grandmother a disco record?
c Why don't you buy your father a gold chain?
d How about buying your little sister a video camera?
e Why don't you send some fruit to your cousin in Australia?
f How about buying your little brother some writing paper?
g What about buying your penfriend a model plane?
h How about giving our teacher some black leather trousers?

SKILLS: LISTENING AND WRITING

Pre-writing

1 Choose the most suitable phrase from each pair underlined.

> Jean
>
> What are you doing/will you do next Wednesday (the 18th)?
> I'm going shopping/I'll go shopping in London. Do you like/
> Would you like to come with me? I think/I'm thinking of getting
> some new camping things, but I'm not sure what to buy. I'm
> needing/I'm going to need some good equipment, because I'll
> go/I'm going camping in the Scottish Highlands this Easter. Tell
> me what you think at the tennis club on Saturday morning. I'll
> see/I'm going to see you there at about 9.30.
>
> Ricky

Writing

2 Write a note from Jean in reply, based on this information.
Choose suitable tenses, and add any necessary words.

> Sorry/ not come/ tennis club/ this Saturday. Take/driving test.
> My mother/ take me/ the test centre 9.00. My test/9.45.
> What/you do/Sunday? How about/go/for a drive? (if I pass!)
> My brother/lend me his car. I/think/go/Brighton/for a swim.
> Dave and Sheila/come to stay this weekend too. I/give/you a
> ring on Friday afternoon.

3 Write a short note like the note in question 1 arranging a meeting
with a friend on Saturday to go shopping. Send the note to
someone.

Write a reply to the note you receive explaining that you can't
meet on Saturday. Arrange another meeting.

Listening

4 🖸 Listen to Ricky and Jean in a shop. Some of the products they
mention are shown here. Tick (✓) the ones they talk about.

5 Imagine you are Jean, and
that you are going camping
in Scotland. Complete this
letter to a friend.

> (your address)
> (the date)
>
> Dear . . . . . ,
> I'm sorry I haven't written
> for so long, but I've been
> really busy. Anyway, I've
> had a great idea for a
> holiday, so I thought of you!
> ....
> (Explain where you are
> going, when, and with
> whom.)
> ....
> (Invite your friend to come
> with you.)
> ....
> (Explain what camping
> equipment you are taking
> with you.)
> ....
> Please write soon and tell me
> if you want to come. I'm sure
> we'll have a really good time.
>
> See you soon,
> Jean

Check your grammar

Talking about the future: *going to* and future use of present continuous, uses of *will*

1 Choose the most suitable response for the sentences.
   a Do you have any plans for the summer? _____
   b Have you decided which train to take? _____
   c How about going sight-seeing tomorrow morning? _____
   d Goodbye, I hope we meet again. _____

   1 I'm leaving on the 8.00 train, actually.
   2 I'll see you in Paris in July.
   3 I'm probably going to stay with some friends in Paris.
   4 Yes, I think I'll catch the 6.30 on Saturday.

Comparatives and superlatives

2 a 'These shoes are more expensive.'
      What are we comparing the shoes with?
      1 One other pair of shoes.
      2 All the other shoes in the shop.
   b 'In fact, these shoes are the most expensive shoes in the shop.'
      What are we comparing the shoes with?
      1 One other pair of shoes.
      2 All the other shoes in the shop.

Build your vocabulary

Compound words

1 Find words which match the definitions. Check in a dictionary whether the new word is written as one word or two.

   a list which you use when you go shopping   *shopping list*

   a clock which rings in the morning   _____

   a machine which makes coffee   _____

   paper used for writing letters   _____

   rings you wear in your ears   _____

   powder used for washing clothes   _____

Word field: shopping

2 Make lists of:
   a six shops
   b four things you can buy in each shop

Practise your pronunciation

Sentence stress

1 ▭ Listen to the sentences below. Each sentence is divided into groups of words, starting from the end of the sentence. Repeat each group of words.
   a Vegetables / are / a lot / cheaper / than meat / in most countries.
   b John and Pete / are having / a party / on Saturday.
   c Excuse me, but / do you / know anywhere / that sells / matches?
   d I'm / looking for / a birthday / present for / a friend of mine.
   e I'll / give you / a ring on / Wednesday evening.

2 ▭ Listen again and circle the syllables that have most stress.

Unit 5   On the road

STARTING POINTS

Road safety

1 Find ten dangers in the picture.

2 Make a list of rules for pedestrians, and a list of rules for drivers.

Pedestrians
Cross the road at traffic lights. It's much safer.
Drivers
Don't enter a main road without stopping and looking both ways.

▶ Interview questions
▶ Present perfect and past simple
▶ Problem situations

International company requires experienced chauffeur for Rolls Royce. Apply in writing to Box 38, The Times, London.

1 Do you know how to drive? What special qualities do you need for a job like this? Could you do it?

Read a letter to a friend from someone who applied for the job. Fill in the information on the job application form below.

> Just a quick note to say that I'll be in London next week. I've applied for a job with a big company, and I'm going to see the transport manager on Thursday (24th). Keep your fingers crossed. Since Lady Barbara decided to drive herself everywhere I've been looking for a job, and that was three months ago. I'm a bit worried about what they'll ask me. Do you remember when I hit that bus in 1986? Still, it wasn't my fault, and it's better to tell the truth. I'm going to explain about the two years I worked as a mechanic as well. After all, I learned a lot about cars. I think that I stand a chance of getting the job. I've got fifteen years' driving experience which is the main thing. . . .

Past simple 2.1

I **passed** my test ten years ago.
I **had** an accident in 1989.

Present perfect simple 3.1

I**'ve had** a licence for ten years.
I**'ve** never **had** an accident.

Application Form

1 Driving licence: years held. ....
2 Accident record. Give details if necessary. ....

Yes No
3 Are you employed at present? ☐ ☐
If *No*, when did you leave your last job? ....

Yes No
4 Any other employment experience? ☐ ☐
If *Yes*, give details. ....

Use the form to decide questions the transport manager can ask John, and give his answers. Use this list to help you.

Have you . . . ?
How long have you . . . ?
Did you . . . ?
When did you . . . ?
Why did you . . . ?
What happened . . . ?

2 You are another candidate for the job. Prepare some details of your driving based on the application form in question 1.

Role play

3

Student A
You are the transport manager. Interview the candidate.

Student B
You are the candidate. Use your notes to answer the questions.

4 Look at the pictures and comments below. Decide when each comment was made, and who is speaking.

Present perfect continuous   3.2

I've been waiting for hours.

Comments

We've run out of petrol.
We forgot the map.
We've forgotten the map.
We've been having problems with the phone recently.
We've been driving around for ages!
We got lost.
We phoned you several times.
We passed that pub an hour ago!
We've been waiting for hours!
We've never got lost before.

5 What can you say in each situation? Talk about what you *did*, what you *have done*, and what you *have been doing*.

A friend wants back the bike you borrowed six weeks ago!
The police want to know why you are driving without a licence.
You promised to repair a friend's car. The friend is still waiting!
The ticket inspector on the train says you have the wrong ticket.
You are very late for your plane. The airline won't let you on.

Role play

6 Act out these situations.

Student A	**Student B**
You are in a motorway restaurant. You are very tired as you have been driving all day. You ordered a meal over half an hour ago but no one has served you yet. Complain to the waiter/waitress.	You are the waiter/waitress. A lot of things have gone wrong today. Explain what has happened or been happening. Try to keep the customer happy.

Student A	**Student B**
You are a hotel owner. You won't give a room to someone who has dirty clothes and no luggage. You think that this person has no money.	You are on a walking holiday. A lot of things have gone wrong and you need a hotel room. Explain what has happened and persuade the hotel owner that you are respectable!

Pre-reading

1 What is your opinion of public transport?

Reading

2 Find information in the text and table and complete each sentence.

   a A journey through Zones 1 and 2 for an adult costs _____ .
   b A child pays _____ to travel any distance at peak times.
   c An adult bus pass for a day in three zones costs _____ .
   d The most expensive ordinary adult fare is _____ and is for _____ zones.
   e A child pays _____ for an Off-Peak 1-Day Travelcard.

BUSES

1 The system of bus fares is based on zones, like Underground fares. If you travel in the rush hour during the 5 week, you may pay more in some zones. Fares are also higher if you are travelling through two or more zones and one of these is Zone 1 (Central London). 10 A journey in the central zone costs 70p, with a journey across three zones costing as much as £1.40, and across two zones between £1.00 and 60p. 15 London Transport can sell you a One Day Bus pass (this does not include the central zone) but it may be better to buy a Travel Card, which you can also use on 20 the Underground and on British Rail.

A One Day Pass is good value for travel by bus outside Zone 1. This costs between £1.10 and £1.90, 25 depending on how many zones you travel in. You can buy Bus Passes in advance from newsagents and some bus garages. If you live in an outer 30 area (for example, Bexley, Surbiton or Croydon), buy a Local Area Bus Pass. This costs £3.60 to travel for a week inside your suburb.

ONE DAY BUS PASSES	ADULT	CHILD
ONE ZONE Zone 2 **OR** Zone 3 Zone 4 (5, 6)	£1.10 £1.25	90p 90p
TWO ZONES Zones 2 and 3 Zones 3 and 4(5,6)	£1.40 £1.40	90p 90p
THREE ZONES Zones 2, 3 and 4(5,6)	£1.90	90p
OFF-PEAK 1-DAY TRAVELCARDS		
TWO ZONES Zones 1, 2*	£2.30	£1.00
FOUR ZONES Zones 1, 2, 3 and 4*	£2.60	£1.00
ALL ZONES Zones 1, 2, 3, 4, 5, 6*	£2.90	£1.00

ORDINARY FARES		ADULT		CHILD	
		Peak*	Off-peak	Peak*	Off-peak
ONE ZONE	including Zone 1 excluding Zone 1	70p 50p	70p 50p	40p 40p	25p 25p
TWO ZONES	including Zone 1 excluding Zone 1	£1 70p	£1 60p	40p 40p	25p 25p
THREE ZONES	including Zone 1 excluding Zone 1	£1.40 £1	£1.10 60p	40p 40p	25p 25p
ALL ZONES		£1.60	£1.10	40p	25p

3 You and your family (two adults, three children) want to go to Wembley Statium (Zone 4) by bus. You are staying in Hammersmith, (Zone 2). What is the lowest cost of tickets for the whole family there and back?

Pre-listening

4 What are the advantages of travelling around a city in these ways? Are there any problems?

by bus   by train or tube   by car   by motorbike

Listening

5 🔲 Listen to two people discussing how they travel in a large city. Before you listen, study the table and predict what they will say. As you listen, write in the table information from the conversation.

	public transport	car
cost		
problems		
convenience		

Do you agree with what they say?

Reading

6 Read the text and decide:

What do you think were the main reasons why Amanda bought the car?
Is she pleased with it?

Comprehension check

7 Find parts of the text which support these statements.

a Amanda wanted to avoid paying a lot of money to run her car.

b Because she had so little money, there were not a lot of cars to choose from.

c She didn't want a large car which would be difficult to park.

d After she went for a drive in a Yugo, she decided to buy one immediately.

e If she sold her car now, she wouldn't get a very good price for it.

Speaking

8 Some people think that using bicycles is a solution to the problem of city transport. What do you think?

---

1 When Amanda Hollings, a 29-year-old English teacher from Aylesbury in Buckinghamshire, decided to treat herself to a
5 brand new car two years ago, she opted for a 903cc Yugo 45A GLS. She wanted a new car so she could save on maintenance bills and MoT test worries.
10   'I didn't have very much money, so there wasn't much choice. I looked at the Mini City E but it was rather basic and I also had a test drive in a Lada
15 Riva but it was too big,' explained Amanda.
   'Then a friend suggested a Yugo. I went along to my local

LIVING WITH A YUGO 45A GLS

dealer and was impressed – the
20 Yugo 45A was the right size, small enough to park easily. I

had a test drive and placed my order the same day.
   'It's quite luxurious, with
25 cloth upholstery and a stereo but it only cost just over £3,500.
   'I still think it's good value for money, though depreciation is quite heavy. It's not worth much
30 now, so I'll be keeping it for a few more years. It's only done 13,000 miles so far and has been reliable and economical with an average of 36mpg.
35   'Would I buy another? Yes, but there's no point – mine is still in lovely condition and I'm sure there are many years left in it yet.'

Present perfect simple ▶ 3.1

1 What do the people say in each situation? Use the verb given.

Jack is running towards the bus stop, but he is too late to catch the bus.   (miss)
Oh bother, I've missed the bus!

a Sheila is in the railway station looking worried. We can see her bag inside the train. The train is moving.   (leave)
b The ticket inspector is talking to Paul. Paul is searching his pockets and looking embarrassed.   (lose)
c Sue and Mark are meeting a friend at the station, but so far there is no sign of the train.   (arrive)
d Bill is at the airport in passport control. He is looking very worried and explaining something to the passport officer.   (forget)
e Sue is at the airport to meet friends. The light on the 'Landed' sign is now on.   (land)
f The driving instructor is shaking hands with George and smiling.   (pass).

Past simple and present perfect simple ▶ 2.1, 3.1

2 Read Sandra's curriculum vitae and comment on the details of her career so far. Use either the present perfect or the past simple form of the verbs given below.

*She **has worked** as a garage mechanic.*   Time not given
*She **studied** engineering from 1979–1983.*   Time given

study   work as   drive   build   win   take part in

Qualifications:
        1979–83 BA Degree in Engineering
        British Motor Racing School Certificate

Experience:
        Garage mechanic (while at school)
        Sales Department, Fast Cars Ltd. (UK)
        In New York for six months.
  1984 Driving instructor (part-time)
        Construction of own racing car
  1985 Team driver, Formula 3
  1986 One victory (Norwich Grand Prix)
  1985–present Racing instructor

Rallies:
        Paris–Dakar, Monte Carlo

Past participles ▶ 3.1, 21

3 Give the past participle for each verb in the list.

eat – *eaten*

eat	lose
steal	find
drink	fall
speak	have
go	write
read	see

4 Use the verbs in question 3 and the word list to ask questions. Give true answers as far as possible.

Have you (ever) eaten fish for breakfast?

fish
a wallet
keys
War and Peace
English
a cold
to England
a nightmare
a rainbow
in love
money
abroad
an octopus
a letter
anything
asleep
your memory
a French film

Present perfect simple and past simple ▶ 3.1, 2.1

5 Choose the best ending for each sentence.

a	I've been waiting for the bus	1	since 1985.
b	I had a very good holiday in France	2	since I left school.
c	I haven't travelled by train	3	for over two hours.
d	I owned a motorbike	4	from 1983 to 1986.
e	The first tourists came here	5	last week.
f	I've finished paying for my car	6	last year.
g	I've been working for this company	7	at last.
h	I finished paying for my car	8	in the 1950s.

Finished or unfinished ▶ 3.1, 3.2

6 For each sentence, decide whether the action is **finished** (f) or **unfinished/likely to continue** (u).

a I've been taking driving lessons since last August.
b I've been parking my car in this car park for the last two years.
c I've painted my old bike red, and now it looks like new.
d I've been selling cars since I joined this firm in 1987.
e I've learned a lot about cars by reading this book.
f They've been painting a new crossing on the road all morning.
g I've sold my car to that chap who lives in the house opposite.
h I've parked the car outside the pub at the end of the road.

Time expressions ▶ 17

7 What do the people in each situation say? Use present perfect simple, present perfect continuous or past simple and time expressions from the list. More than one answer may be possible.

lately	since (date)
for ages	just
recently	all morning/
for (period	afternoon/
of time)	day/night

Keith is sitting at his desk drinking coffee, looking tired. It is six o'clock in the morning.

I've been studying all night.
I've finished my work at last!

a Jean is holding a letter and looking very happy.
b Gordon is looking very frightened.
c Brian is very muddy, and arriving home wearing his football kit.
d David looks fat and his clothes are too small for him.
e Sheila is waiting at the bus stop and looking at her watch.
f Nick looks tired, he is stretching and getting out of his car.
g Sue is waking Jack who was asleep in front of the television.

Vocabulary

1 Study the picture of the car below. Fill in as many words as you can on the picture.

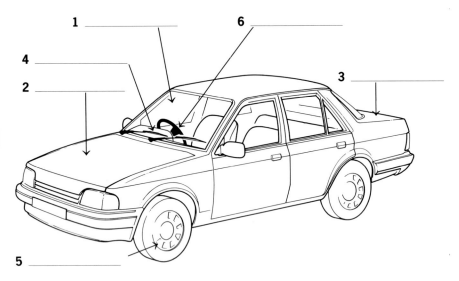

Listening

2 🖭 Listen to extracts from a story. In the story, some parts of a car are mentioned. As you listen, fill in the words on the picture.

3 You have heard some parts of the story. What do you think happened in the complete story? Tell the story from the beginning.

Pre-writing

4 Some of these sentences belong to the story. Decide which ones are suitable.

  a We managed to pull the other car to a nearby pub.
  b We put all the suitcases into the boot and drove on.
  c It was difficult to drive fast, because I couldn't see very well.
  d It was raining hard and the road was very dangerous.
  e A policeman helped us to start the car and we continued our journey.
  f I just managed to stop in time.
  g 'The car broke down, and I decided to sleep in it for the night.'
  h The car crashed into a tree and the driver was injured.
  i The driver was looking under the bonnet with a torch.
  j 'Do you need any help?'

Writing

5 Write the story. The pictures below give the beginning and the end.

6 Plan a similar story beginning with **one** of the sentences below and tell the story. Divide your story into two parts:

the main events
a break-down, an accident, getting lost
the outcome
what happened in the end

Recently I decided to buy a car so I started having driving lessons.
Last year my parents bought me a motor-bike.
For the past month I've been riding my bike to school/work.

Give your story a title, and write two paragraphs.

Check your grammar

Present perfect simple, present perfect continuous, past simple

1 Match each sentence to the diagram which best explains the tense used.

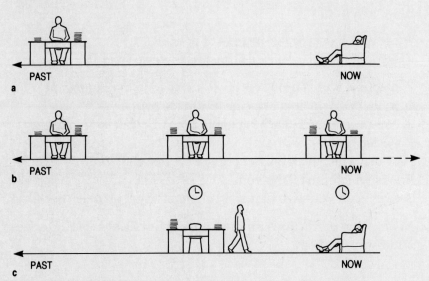

PAST   NOW

a

PAST   NOW

b

PAST   NOW

c

I stopped work an hour ago.
I've stopped work.
I've been working all day.

2 How do you say the sentences in question 1 in your language? What difference is there in the way English and your language express each one?

Build your vocabulary

Word field: on the road

1 Divide this list into three groups of words, with these headings. Use a dictionary if necessary.

using a car   **using a motorbike**   **walking in the street**

Write a sentence or make a drawing to help you remember each word.

seat belt	boot	wheel	brake
gloves	crash-helmet	crossing	steering-wheel
pedestrian	pavement		

2 Add other words you know to the groups you made.

Practise your pronunciation

Spelling and sounds

1 The system of spelling in English can trick you into making mistakes in pronunciation. Decide how to say each group of words.

  a whistle   listen   castle
  b wonderful   gloves mother
  c village   luggage sausage
  d could   would   should
  e comb   lamb   thumb

  ☎ Listen and repeat.

2 Can you add any more words to these groups? Can you make any other groups?

Unit 6 Looking forward

STARTING POINTS

Life in the future

1 Imagine that you live in the year 2100. The inventions described below are now in use. Describe why they are useful. Add two more inventions.

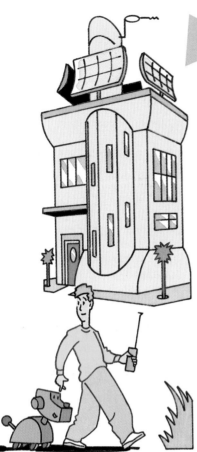

A car which uses water instead of petrol.
This is very useful, because now there isn't any petrol left.

A machine which produces any kind of food that you want.
A robot dog which guards the house for you.
A computer which teaches people how to speak languages perfectly.
A house which uses only energy from the sun.
Books which can talk to you.
A television with two thousand channels from all over the world.

2 Make some predictions for the future about these topics. Discuss and compare them.

LANGUAGE ACTIVITIES

▶ Making predictions about yourself
▶ Making predictions about society
▶ Acting for the future

1 Do you ever think about your future? What things in your life do you think will change?

These pictures show a person's life now, and the future for the same person at different ages. Make some predictions for each one.

> **Future time clause   5.4**
>
> ***When she is** 35, I expect **she'll be in charge** of the company.*

> **Future of prediction   4.1**
>
> *I hope **I'll** be rich.*
> *He **won't dress** in the same way.*
> *I don't think **she'll look** the same.*
>
> **Future continuous   4.3**
>
> *I'll still **be studying** English.*

In 5 years' time
I'll be living.....
I'll be working....
and in my spare
time I'll be....

Now

At the moment I'm single, and I live at home with my parents. I work in an office as a trainee manager, but the job is not very interesting. I also study in my spare time. I don't earn a lot at the moment, so I don't have a car. Some friends of mine have a rock band and I spend the rest of my free time singing with them.

In 5 years' time

In 10 years' time

In 20 years' time

Role play

2 Write a brief self-portrait, like the one in question 1. Give this to a partner.

Student A	Student B
Make some predictions about your partner for five, ten and twenty years time based on the text you read.	Agree or disagree, saying how you feel and what you think is possible. Give your own predictions.

3 Are you an optimist or a pessimist? Do you think that life will be easier or harder in the future?

Do you agree with these predictions for the future? Make some predictions about the topics given below, either agreeing or disagreeing.

> ### *Future Trends*
>
> *And what of the city of the future? Most futurologists agree that there will be **too many** people in large cities, that there wo**n't** be **enough** houses for everyone, and that almost certainly there will be **too much** noise and pollution. People will have to live on pills, because there won't be enough food, and they won't be able to choose where they live …*

city life   home life   work and leisure

What do you think it will be like in your country in 100 years' time?

4 What should we do now, to make sure that the future will be a place worth living in?

*If we **plant** more trees now, the people in the future **will have** a better environment and **there won't be** problems with the weather.*

action now	future result
Plant more trees.	No problems with the weather. Enough water for everyone. A place for everyone to live. No more starving people. Cleaner air, no pollution. Cures for all diseases. No shortage of energy. Enough food and living space.

Future of prediction

With have to, be able to

People **will be able to** work at home.
We **will have to** save water.

Too much, too many, not enough   13.2

Much is used with uncountable nouns (words which do not have plurals).
too much **noise**
Many is used with countable nouns.
too many **cars**
Not enough is used with both countable and uncountable nouns.
not enough **houses**
not enough **money**

Conditional 1: real situations   5.1

If we **take care** of the environment our children **will have** a better future.

48

Pre-reading

1 How do you think some everyday objects might change in the future? Use the list below to make some predictions.

Perhaps we'll be able to see the person we talk to on the phone.

telephone   television   radio   cooker   camera   watch

Reading

2 Read the instruction leaflet for a type of phone now common in Britain. What is different about it?

Comprehension check

3 Study the leaflet and answer the questions below.

a Can money be used for making phone calls from this type of phone?

b Do you have to put in a card if you want to make a 999 call?

c Can you make more than one call with the same card?

d If your card runs out during a call, do you have to ring off?

e What do you have to do to get your card back at the end of the call?

f Is it possible to find out if your card has unused units on it?

g What should you do with your card when all the units are finished?

h Where should you take your card if something is wrong with it?

How to use your Phonecard

Phonecard phones will accept only British Telecom Phonecards, NOT telephone credit cards, other credit cards, or coins.

Emergency '999' calls, which are free of charge, can be made from Phonecard phones, but not other operator connected calls.

Phonecards have tracks of call charge units which are erased automatically from the card during the call. The 20, 40 and 100 unit cards have a single track. The 200 unit card has 2 tracks of 100 units each which can be used in any order. It is not necessary to use one track completely before starting on the other.

1. Lift the receiver and listen for dial tone (continuous purring or new dial tone – a high pitched hum).

2. Insert the card into the slot, green side up, in the direction of the arrow, and press it fully home.

3. Dial the number you want. The digital display will show the number of unused units on the card (or on the track actually inserted in the case of a 200 unit card). Listen for the ringing tone and speak when connected. The credit units are progressively erased as shown on the digitial display.

Follow-on calls.

If you have unused units remaining on a card and you wish to make a new call, do not replace the receiver. Instead, briefly depress and release the receiver rest. As soon as you hear the dial tone again, you can make your next call.

Using a new card during a call.
Shortly before the units on the card or track are used up the display will begin to flash and an expiry tone (rapid pips) will be heard. If you wish to continue your call with a new card (or the other track of a 200 unit card), press the button situated directly above the card slot: the display will stop flashing, the Phonecard phone will memorise the remaining units and eject the card. Retrieve the card and insert a new one (or an unused track of a 200 unit card). These operations will not interrupt your call.

4. When you finish your call, replace the receiver and the card will be ejected automatically.

5. Retrieve the card.

If at any time you want to know the number of unused units left on a card/track, simply insert it into a Phonecard phone, without lifting the receiver, and the number of remaining units will be shown on the display for a few seconds before the card is ejected automatically. Once you have used all the credit units on your card it cannot be re-used. Please dispose of it carefully in a proper litter container. Keep Britain Tidy.

If a card proves defective it should be returned to British Telecom (our offices are listed in the telephone directory) and NOT to any other Phonecard outlet.

Phonecards should be protected against excessive scratching or soiling and, when not in use, should always be kept in the plastic Phonecard wallet supplied with every Phonecard issued.

Reading

4 Scan the text and find what the customers are drinking, and why. Is this in the future?

Inhale and Hearty

1 Oxygen's a tonic in this revolutionary bar.

Feeling in need of a tonic? Why not take a deep breath of tasty-flavoured oxygen? It's guaranteed, so they say, to sharpen you up and put you in good shape for the rest of the day.

5 If the idea has a dash of Far-Eastern promise about it, then it's probably because the be-inhale-and-hearty fad has taken off at Tokyo's Takashimaya department store. At a special bar, customers can get a three-minute shot of oxygen for around 50p.

There are four flavours to make the whole experience plea-

10 santly stimulating – there's lemon, mint, coffee and a rather delicious mushroom odour. Wafting its way on the menu shortly will be orange flavour.

The flavour is produced when the appropriate extract is dropped into the mouthpiece. Then the customers, who flock to

15 the bar from miles around, inhale the stimulating intake.

With a strong yen to cash in on the Christmas gifts trade, the store is now selling canned oxygen from between £8 to £12 – prices guaranteed to take your breath away!

Word search

5 Find words or phrases in the article which could be replaced by the words or phrases below.

a a health medicine	**e** smell
b put you in good condition	**f** breathe in
c fashion	**g** desire to make money from
d has become popular	**h** give you a shock

6 The words and phrases **a** to **e** are difficult words from the text. Study the text where they appear, and match them to the explanations **1** to **5**. One phrase given is not exactly the same in the text. Can you say why?

a a yen
b flock
c hale and hearty
d stimulating
e a shot

1 a small amount of an alcoholic drink
2 a Japanese unit of currency
3 making more active
4 in good health
5 go in large numbers

Pre-listening

7 What other everyday activities will change in the future? Make one prediction for each topic.

computers
energy
animals
clothes
shopping
leisure
entertainment
money
houses

Listening

8 📼 As you listen, make brief notes of the topics mentioned, and the predictions made. Decide whether you agree with the predictions.

Countables and uncountables ▶ 15

1 Which words in the list are countable and which are uncountable?

countable	an exercise
	some exercises
	exercises
uncountable	_____
	some money
	_____

furniture	news
hair	English
information	journey
luggage	progress
trousers	travel
knowledge	exercise
advice	money

2 Complete each sentence with a word from the list. Use a plural form if necessary.

animal	car
food	house
free time	money
traffic	work

a There won't be enough _____ for some people.

b There will probably be too much _____ in large cities.

c I think there will be too few _____ left in the world.

d I expect there will be too many _____ everywhere.

e Most of the time there won't be enough _____ for everyone.

f The police will have too little _____ to do.

Articles ▶ 16

3 Do you agree or disagree with these predictions? Put *a/an* or *the* into each space where necessary.

a _____ rock group from _____ Soviet Union will have _____ world-wide hit.

b _____ students in my country will learn _____ Chinese at _____ school.

c Someone in _____ class will get _____ job as _____ English teacher.

d _____ Iceland will win _____ Eurovision Song Contest.

e Someone in _____ school will play _____ guitar in _____ rock concert.

f _____ school will organise _____ trip by _____ bus to _____ England.

g _____ present _____ Prime Minister will win _____ next election.

h _____ most people in this class will pass _____ exam in _____ June.

i _____ Saturday's match will be _____ better than _____ last week's.

j _____ English will become _____ most popular language in _____ world.

Conditional 1 ▶ 5.1

4 Make a prediction beginning *If . . .* for each situation. There are two ways of making predictions for some situations.

It's going to rain! You'll get wet! Take an umbrella!
***If you take** an umbrella, **you won't get** wet.*
***If you don't take** an umbrella, **you'll get** wet!*

a You're eating too much! You're going to put on weight!

b Hurry up! We're going to miss the train!

c United need to score a goal now to win the match!

d Don't touch the dog! It always bites people!

e Drive faster! We want to arrive home before 6.00.

f Turn the oven off! You might burn the food.

g You have to study hard to pass the examination!

h Read the instructions. They tell you what to do.

Future time clauses ▶ 5.4

5 Put each verb in brackets into either present simple, present perfect or *will* form.

  a I (send) you a letter as soon as I (receive) the tickets.
  b When the play (finish), we (go) to a restaurant.
  c Don't worry, I (wait) here until you (come) back.
  d I (return) your book after I (finish) this chapter.
  e I (give) you a ring when I (get) home from work.
  f We (come) and see you again before we (leave).
  g As soon as we (have) any news, we (let) you know.
  h I think I (stay) indoors until my cold (get) better.

Text organisers

6 Read the text carefully and choose which word or phrase is best. What do you think? Have you any proof that horoscopes actually work?

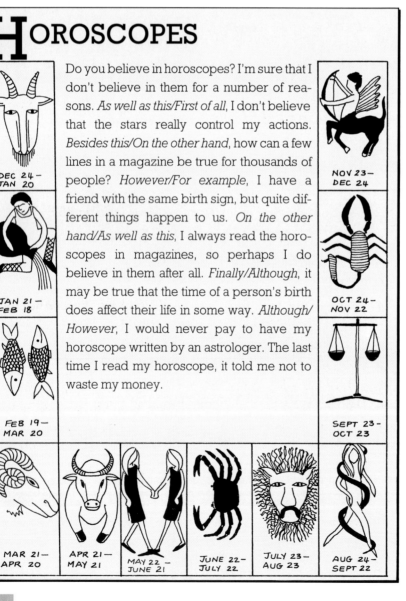

Horoscopes

Do you believe in horoscopes? I'm sure that I don't believe in them for a number of reasons. *As well as this/First of all*, I don't believe that the stars really control my actions. *Besides this/On the other hand*, how can a few lines in a magazine be true for thousands of people? *However/For example*, I have a friend with the same birth sign, but quite different things happen to us. *On the other hand/As well as this*, I always read the horoscopes in magazines, so perhaps I do believe in them after all. *Finally/Although*, it may be true that the time of a person's birth does affect their life in some way. *Although/However*, I would never pay to have my horoscope written by an astrologer. The last time I read my horoscope, it told me not to waste my money.

DEC 24 – JAN 20
JAN 21 – FEB 18
FEB 19 – MAR 20
NOV 23 – DEC 24
OCT 24 – NOV 22
SEPT 23 – OCT 23

MAR 21 – APR 20
APR 21 – MAY 21
MAY 22 – JUNE 21
JUNE 22 – JULY 22
JULY 23 – AUG 23
AUG 24 – SEPT 22

7 Read the sentences, and pay attention to the words underlined. Put the sentences into a logical order so that they make a paragraph. The first two sentences are in the correct position.

CANCER

June 22nd to July 22nd

This is a great time for you! <u>First of all</u>, you will find the confidence you need to make progress at work. <u>On the other hand</u>, a friend will misunderstand you in a number of ways. <u>However</u>, at home things won't go quite so well, but be patient. <u>Finally</u>, take extra care if you go on a journey between the 14th and the 25th when the moon moves into your sign. <u>As well as this</u>, they will try to understand you at last. <u>For example</u>, you could argue about money,

so be careful. <u>Although</u> loved ones may prove difficult, you will find that if you wait they will need your help towards the end of the month.

SKILLS: LISTENING AND WRITING

Listening

1 🔲 Listen to parts of a radio programme in which a panel of experts talk about the future. Identify the topic each expert is talking about by choosing **a**, **b** or **c**.

Professor Graham
a health **b** controlling traffic **c** crime

Dr Nicholson
a space flight **b** holidays and travel **c** city life

Keith Deacon
a housework **b** business **c** factories

Judith Graves
a shopping **b** work **c** studying

2 🔲 Listen again and decide whether these statements about the talk are **true** (t) or **false** (f).

a Professor Graham says that we'll be able to see new places.
b Professor Graham says that lives will be saved.
c Dr Nicholson thinks that transport will be different.
d Dr Nicholson says that things will improve in the end.
e Keith Deacon says that his wife will answer the phone.
f Keith Deacon says that the computer will tell lies if necessary.
g Judith Graves says that writing letters will be easier.
h Judith Graves says that spelling will not be a problem.

Pre-writing

3 Read the text and the list of text organisers. Put one organiser into each gap in the text. Use each one once only.

as as well as this because finally first of all however
on the other hand so

[1] _____, I won't be in exactly the same job. [2] _____, I expect I'll be doing the same kind of job, [3] _____ it is difficult to change career. [4] _____, I'll still be a teacher, but I hope I'll be a head-teacher. [5] _____, I expect I'll be living in a large city, not in my home town. I think it will probably be a very crowded and dirty place. [6] _____, I expect I'll be able to have long holidays in the mountains, [7] _____ people will have a lot of free time in the future. [8] _____, I expect I'll be earning more money than I do now.

4 Read these notes for a composition with the title:

How do you imagine the future?

Divide the notes into three parts, so that you have material for three different paragraphs. Give each paragraph a title.

I hope I'll have a good job.
There will be too many people.
More people will leave villages.
I hope I'll be happy.
I expect I'll be married.
Perhaps we will find a solution.
My country will be different.
People will be living on the moon.
There will be a shortage of food.
We will have better roads.
I'll speak English well.
The poor countries will be poorer.
Most people will be better off.
I'll have a lot of good friends.
There will be more tourists here.
I'll be living in a large city.

Writing

5 Make your own notes for the composition. Discuss the topic before writing. Write three paragraphs. Include text organisers from question 3 where possible.

Check your grammar

Articles

1 Choose the correct version of the sentence and explain the use of the article.

I bought **some** furniture.
Furniture is uncountable. Indefinite article (a/an) is not used with uncountable nouns.

  a I bought some furniture/I bought a furniture.
  b The swimming is easy/Swimming is easy.
  c She is engineer/She is an engineer.
  d He is learning the piano/He is learning piano.
  e The criminal spent ten years in prison/in the prison.
  f Don't wake her, she's in the bed/in bed.
  g I visited the France and the United States/France and United States/France and the United States.

Sentences with *If . . .*

2 Which sentences make a **prediction**, and which ones describe **what always happens**? Underline the verbs used in each sentence.
  a If you press this button, the machine stops.
  b If you are not careful, you will fall in the water.
  c If she slips, she'll break her leg.
  d If you put this in water, it turns blue.
  e If you ask her nicely, she'll give you a lift home.

Build your vocabulary

Adjectives ending -*ing*/-*ed*

1 Complete each sentence with the most suitable word given in each pair.
  a I had a very _____ day, so I went to bed early.   tired/tiring
  b I was rather _____ by the film, so I left.   bored/boring
  c I enjoyed reading the article, it was very _____ .   stimulated/stimulating
  d She is very _____ in architecture.   interested/interesting.
  e After getting his letter I felt _____ .   worried/worrying

2 Which of the words in question 1 describe **how people feel**, and which ones describe **how people feel about something**?

Practise your pronunciation

Intonation

1 ▭ Listen and repeat what each speaker says. Try to imitate their intonation.

  a Hi, are you enjoying the party?
  b Your name's Sue, isn't it?
  c Do you think I could have some more Coke?
  d What's the name of that boy over there?
  e Where's the ice?

2 Study these questions, and decide how you would say them. The situation is given for each speaker.

  a Have you got any more coffee?
      (polite, in a friend's house)
  b Do you think I could use the phone?
      (polite, when visiting an office)
  c Would you like to dance?
      (to someone you have just met)
  d What's the English word for this?
      (to your teacher in the class)
  e Are you sitting here?
      (to a stranger on a train)

▭ Listen and repeat.

Unit 7 The time of your life

Taking a holiday

1 What are the advantages and the disadvantages of the holidays shown in these advertisements?

2 Use the table to plan the holiday you are going to have this year.

name of place	
number of days	
number of people	
method of travel	
accommodation	

Describe your holiday plan, and give the reasons for your choices.

▶ Choosing a holiday
▶ Giving advice
▶ Holiday problems

1 What kinds of holidays are shown in the pictures? Why do people go on each kind of holiday?

1   2

What kind of holiday is each person describing?

Brenda Jackson: *We always come here to relax. I don't have to worry about my work, and it's a real break. We usually spend about two weeks in different places so that the children can see something interesting, and keep busy!*

Gareth Price   *I'm a student so this kind of holiday suits me best, it's not too expensive and most of my friends enjoy this kind of thing. We usually bring our guitars so that we can do some singing and dancing. It's great as long as it doesn't rain!*

What kind of holiday is best for these people? Give reasons for each person.

A family with four children.
A single person.
A group of school friends who don't have much money.
A very busy business man or woman.

2 Read these advertisements. What do you think are the good and bad points of these holidays? Add two more ideas for an unusual holiday.

Live for two weeks on your own desert island in the Pacific . . .

Jungle safari – the holiday of a lifetime . . .

Stay with an Eskimo family in the frozen Arctic . . .

Infinitive of purpose   12.1
*We go there **to relax**.*

Purpose clause   12.2
*We bring our guitars **so that we can** do some singing and dancing.*

3

4

Certainty   10.2
*This kind of holiday **must be** expensive.*
*Camping in the jungle **can't be** very comfortable.*

3 Do you take a lot of luggage with you when you go on holiday? Do you think that it is a good idea to take these things with you? Think of five more useful things.

Advise others to take the items shown, and the ones on your list, with them on holiday. Explain why you think they should take these things.

What might go wrong on a holiday? Make a list of six points and discuss them.

4 What holiday problems are shown here?

What kinds of holidays do people have in your own country? Do they ever have any problems?

Giving advice 8.2, 9.4
You had (you'd) better take a blanket.   **You ought to** take some books.   **You should** take some food.

Possibility 10.1
It **could** be very cold.   You **might** feel bored.   You **might not like** the local food.

Too and *not enough* 13.2
It was **too expensive**. We couldn't afford to eat!   The sea was**n't warm enough** for me!

Result clauses 13.1
Sometimes it's **so crowded that** you can't find a hotel room.

Role play

5

Student A	**Student B**
You want some information and advice about holidays in Student B's country, or part of the country. Ask about: ● How to get there, the best forms of transport. ● Where to go, places of interest, beaches. ● Where to stay, what to eat, any problems. ● Money and prices, what to avoid.	Give as much information as possible. Give information about: ● A place you know well, a holiday you took yourself. ● Recommend the best places to visit. ● Give some advice about what to take with you, what to avoid.

Pre-reading

1 If you were going to visit a historic city, what kinds of places would you expect to see? What else would you do while you were there?

Reading

2 Read the text and find this information about the city of York.

YORK QUIZ

1 Where can you find the following?

  a The shape of an animal cut on a hill.
  b A street which shows how people used to live in the past.
  c Information about submarines.
  d A very large building built in the middle ages.

2 Which places **can't** you visit at these times?

  a Weekdays at 10.00am
  b Sundays at 10.00am
  c Any day at 6.30pm
  d Mondays in March

3 How much does it cost for a family of two adults and two children to visit all the places mentioned?

YORK
CITY OF LIVING HISTORY

What To See

1 The Minister. York's cathedral is the largest medieval building in Britain, now restored after the freak storm which damaged it in 1984. See the
5 astronomical clock, dedicated to the thousands of airmen who died in World War II and the Five Sisters window, which is as big as a tennis court. Holy Trinity Church in Goodramgate
10 is tiny. Built between 1250 and 1500 its floor has now sunk into the ground but still supports the 18th-century pews.
York Castle Museum tel:0904
15 653611, opposite Clifford's Tower, is the best ever. Its extensive displays of everyday life from the 1800s until today are popular with young and old alike. The most famous attractions
20 are Kirkdale Street and Half Moon Court, a Victorian and Edwardian street respectively, which have been reconstructed in perfect detail. Open Monday – Saturday, 9.30am–5.30pm;
25 Sunday 10am–5.30pm. Adults £2.70; children and pensioners £1.35.
Yorvik Viking Centre, Coppergate tel: 0904 643211, offers a journey back to the tenth century. It's built on the site
30 of the excavation of a Viking street and is a reconstruction of that street. You can experience for yourself how the Vikings lived, worked, ate and even smelled! Open daily 9am–7pm.
35 Adults £2.75; children £1.35.
National Railway Museum, Leeman Road, tel: 0904 621261, 10 minutes' walk from York station. Open Monday–Saturday 10am–6pm, Sunday
40 11am–6pm. Adults £2; children and pensioners £1.
The Shambles, one of the best-preserved medieval streets in Europe, formerly the street of the butchers
45 and now packed with a variety of pretty shops.

Round and About

The lovely country north of York is teeming with historical sites and places.
50 Wharram Percy, known as the lost village. Close to the village of Wharram le Street, off the B1248. Only the church is left but it still builds up a vivid picture of life in the Middle Ages.
55 Eden Camp, tel: 0653 697777, in Old Malton, off the A64, is a living museum showing life during World War II. Displays include being in a U-boat under attack, the Blitz, and fashions
60 of the Forties. Open daily from 10am–5pm. Adults £3.00; children and pensioners £1.50.
Rievaulx Abbey (by the B1257, off the A170). Yorkshire born former Prime
65 Minister Harold Wilson took his title Lord Wilson of Rievaulx from here. This is one of the finest monastic ruins in Britain, full of atmosphere.
The White Horse of Kilburn. The horse
70 is 314 feet long and 228 feet high and was carved out of the chalky hillside by a local schoolmaster in 1857. The horse is best appreciated from a distance on the A1 or A19, or take the 1½
75 mile White Horse Walk – part of the Cleveland Way, which circles the horse.
Yorkshire Museum of Farming, Murton, tel: 0904 489666. An
80 award-winning interpretation of Yorkshire's farming heritage. Open 10.30am–5.30pm daily but closed on Mondays in March, April and October. Adults, £2; pensioners, £1.25, chil-
85 dren £1; family, £5.

Word search

3 Try to guess these words and phrases from the text in A by matching each one with a suitable explanation from B.

A
freak
dedicated
pews
pensioners
packed with
teeming with
the Blitz
monastic ruins
appreciated
heritage

B
the remains of a monastery
people who have retired
offered in memory of
admired
wooden seats in a church
bombing of Britain in World War 2
crowded with
things given from past times
extremely unusual
very full of

Comprehension check

4 Decide whether this information is **given** in the text (g) or **suggested** (s).

a The Cathedral has been repaired since the storm in 1984.
b York Castle museum contains a lot of details about ordinary life in the past.
c The city of York used to be a Viking city.
d The National Railway Museum is close to the railway station.
e Wharram Percy no longer exists as a village with a population.

5 Which of the places in the text would you like to visit in York? Give your reasons.

Listening

6 📼 Listen to a radio programme which gives information about restaurants and hotels in York, and how to get there. Fill in the missing information.

WHERE TO EAT

The Rose Restaurant   about £10.50 each
The Holly Tree   _____
The Queen's Head   _____

WHERE TO STAY

The Galaxy Hotel   For two nights or more, per night:
    _____ incl. dinner and breakfast
    _____ bed and breakfast only
York Manor Hotel   _____ bed and breakfast
The White Horse Hotel   For two to four nights:
    _____ incl. dinner and breakfast
The Old Mill Hotel   _____ bed and breakfast

HOW TO GET THERE

By road, on the _____, _____, and M62. There are airports at _____, Bradford and Humberside. Also excellent rail links with London, _____, Birmingham and the South West.

Possibility and certainty ▶ 10

1 Read the advertisement for a package holiday.

> # ROUND BRITAIN BY BUS
>
> See Britain by luxury 55-seater coach. Ten nights in star hotels, with all meals included. Eleven glorious days of travel, from London to Scotland, Wales, the Lake District, the West Country and all the beauty spots of traditional Britain. Cities visited include: Cambridge, York, Durham, Edinburgh, Inverness, Glasgow, Stratford, Oxford, Bristol and Salisbury. Special rates for students and senior citizens. Sorry, no children under ten.

Imagine that you are thinking of going on this holiday. Use the cues given and the words in the list to make sentences about the trip.

might   could   must   can't   might not

expensive/be
It can't be very expensive to see Britain this way.

a interesting/be
b bus/break down
c people/friendly/be
d drive/fast
e trip/well-organised/be
f ticket/cheap/be
g crowded/be
h foreign tourists/like
i tired/get
j hotels/uncomfortable/be
k places/see/properly
l sick/feel

Obligation ▶ 9

2 Match each sentence with a suitable comment which explains what is said. More than one answer may be possible.

Don't talk to the driver while he is driving.
You are not allowed to.

a *There's no smoking on the bus.*
b *It's not necessary to give a tip.*
c *Stop being so rude to everybody!*
d *Don't throw rubbish out the window!*
e *The rule says KEEP TO THE PATH.*
f *Go and see Shakespeare's house.*
g *The maid will make the beds.*
h *Don't miss the Lake District.*

1 I think you really should!
2 This notice says it's not allowed.
3 Guests don't have to do this.
4 You're not allowed to.
5 You really mustn't do things like that.
6 ... so you have to do this.
7 You really mustn't!
8 It says that we don't have to.

Purpose clauses ▶ 12

3 Write a new sentence using the words given which explains the purpose of each action. Use *so that, could* or infinitive where possible.

I get out/buy souvenirs.
*I got out **to buy** some souvenirs.*

a I phone the receptionist/ask what time the bus leaves.
b The passengers have an afternoon shopping/the driver have a rest.
c An Italian gives me his camera/I take a picture of him.
d We queue for half an hour/we get tickets for *Hamlet*.
e The driver takes us to Loch Ness/we look for the monster.
f The hotel serves us dinner early/we go Scottish country dancing.
g The driver stops/he asks a policeman for directions.
h One of the passengers collects money/we buy the driver a present.
i The guide puts up a list in the hotel/we sign our names for the trip.
j I go on a river trip in Oxford/I see the colleges.

So, too, such and enough ▶ 13.1, 13.2

4 Put one of these words in each space:

so   such   too   enough

I enjoyed the tour on the whole, but by the time I got back I was
[1] _____ tired that I didn't go out for a week. We saw
[2] _____ many castles and churches that I can't remember
which is which. And the trip was [3] _____ fast really. The stops
weren't long [4] _____ for us to see places properly, and some of
the other passengers were [5] _____ busy taking photographs to
look for themselves. It was [6] _____ a long trip that we got
rather tired of travelling after a few days. We were on the bus for
[7] _____ many hours a day that I began to feel sick. The bus
wasn't really comfortable [8] _____, and I was [9] _____ shy to
complain to the guide. But it was [10] _____ a good way of
seeing the country quickly, that I don't really regret taking the
trip.

It and there ▶ 20

5 Complete each sentence with either *it* or *there*.

_____ is a castle near here.
There is a castle near here.

[1] _____ is a lovely square in the centre of the town. [2] _____
is a beautiful place, and many tourists go there. [3] _____ isn't
very far, and you can take a bus. When [4] _____ is raining, of
course, things aren't so good. The tourists usually sit in the cafes
if [5] _____ is nothing else to do. Personally, I don't think
[6] _____ is much point in visiting the local museum. [7] _____
is an interesting stuffed elephant, but not much else. [8] _____
should be more things here for tourists to do, I suppose. But
[9] _____ is all right when the sun is shining. [10] _____ is a
good beach nearby, and you can go windsurfing.

Phrasal/multi-word verbs ▶ 19

6 Put one of the verbs below
into each space.

got up   looking forward to
passed out   pick up
put me up   run out of
ring you up   turn up
wake up   went off

I'm sorry I didn't [1] _____
to catch the train on
Saturday, but something
terrible happened to me. I
[2] _____ late because I
didn't [3] _____ when my
alarm clock [4] _____, and
as I had [5] _____ coffee, I
went down to the corner
shop. Then I realised I'd
forgotten to [6] _____ my
keys, so I decided to break a
window and climb in.
However, I cut myself really
badly and [7] _____. An
ambulance took me to
hospital, and then my sister
told the doctor that she
would [8] _____ for the
night. I know I didn't
[9] _____ but I was
unconscious most of the time!
I'm really sorry, because I
was [10] _____ going to
Scotland.

SKILLS: LISTENING AND WRITING

Listening

1 📻 Listen to four people describing their holidays. Tick (✓) the holidays which your hear mentioned.

2 📻 Listen again and tick (✓) any good points, and problems, which are mentioned by the speakers.

a Freedom to do what you want.
b Good restaurants and hotels.
c Accommodation next to the beach.
d Good for young children.
e Economical and convenient.
f Good way of making friends.

g Home-sickness and loneliness.
h Language problems.
i No water or electricity.
j Problems with insects.
k Too many other people.
l Getting lost.

3 Which holiday in question 1 would you most like to go on? What are the advantages of this kind of holiday? Can you think of any problems you might have?

Pre-writing

4 Study this list of points which could be included in a composition with the title:

A Holiday Which Went Wrong

Choose some of the points below to include in your composition.

deciding where to go	the weather
who you went with	an accident
how you travelled	getting lost
describing the journey there	losing something
where you stayed	solving the problems
places you visited	travelling home

5 Use the points you have chosen to make a plan for a composition with three paragraphs. Give each part of the plan a title. Exchange plans.

Writing

6 Can you use any of these phrases in your story? Tell your story to someone else.

There was only one thing we could do.
Secondly, the weather was very bad.
I haven't been back there since.
In the end we decided to go home.
A few years ago I decided to go to . . .
On the other hand, it was very cheap.
I didn't take enough money.
Then I had a good idea.
I was looking forward to it.
We arrived there on Monday.
The people were very friendly.
Then I noticed it was missing.

Write your story.

Check your grammar

Obligation and certainty

1 Choose the best explanation for each sentence.

a You must be here by nine at the latest.
  1 This is an order. 2 This is certain.
b I think that United could win the match.
  1 This is possible. 2 This is certain.
c Sorry, but you can't use the phone.
  1 This is an order. 2 This is certain.
d You must be John's younger brother.
  1 This is an order. 2 This is certain.
e She could swim when she was five years old.
  1 She was able to. 2 She wanted to.
f This can't be your coat, it's much too small.
  1 This is not possible. 2 This is not allowed.

Build your vocabulary

Words with more than one meaning

1 Many words have more than one meaning. Use a dictionary to find two meanings for each of the words in the list. Note the part of speech (verb, noun) of the words. Write a sentence for each one which makes the meaning clear.

coach (n) *We went to the seaside by coach, not by train.*
coach (v) *Terry coaches the local basketball team.*

rest	change	strike	bark	drop
fair	file	jam	lift	mean

Word Field: holidays

2 This list contains words connected with three different kinds of holidays: **camping** or **walking**, **seaside** and **sight-seeing**. Divide the list into three groups of words. Add any more words you know to each group.

compass	map	tent	coach	guide
sun bathing	tour	sand	museum	sleeping bag
boots	beach	queue	sun tan	sandals

Practise your pronunciation

Spelling and sounds

1 a How would you pronounce these words?

chemistry	jealous
listen	weight
leather	picture
technical	doubt
furniture	neighbour

b Group the words into five pairs. Each pair has a similar problem. The spelling gives a misleading idea of the sound.
🔊 Listen and repeat.

2 How would you pronounce these words? They have one sound in common. What is it?

love	onion
mother	company
London	blood
other	wonderful
become	suddenly

🔊 Listen and repeat.

Unit 8 Meet the family

Family life

1 Describe each member of the family in the cartoon. How do you think they get on with each other?

2 Describe what it is like in these family situations.

Your grandparents live with you and your family.
You are a teenager and your parents are very strict.
You are a young mother with several small children.
You are an old person and you live on your own.
You have six brothers and sisters.

LANGUAGE ACTIVITIES

▶ Reported statements

1 What do people in the same family usually disagree about? Suggest four things.

Who are the people shown in the situations below? Where are they? What is happening?

What words are the people in the situations saying? Match these words with the speakers.

'Don't worry, we know how to do it.'
'I'll be back at 11.30.'
'It's all right, I've started the cooking.'
'We're going to do it before you come home.'

These pictures show the same situations a few hours later. What are the angry people saying?

Reported statements   7.1

Direct speech

'I'll be back at 11.30, Mum.'
'You came home late last night.'

Reported speech

*She said **she would be back** at 11.30.*
*They said **she had come** home late the night before.*

Tell and say   7.3

Direct speech
'I know how to do it.'

Reported speech

*You **told me** you **knew** how to do it.*
*You **said** you **knew** how to do it!*

Role play

2 Take the roles in one of the pictures in question 1 and argue about the situation.

Student A	Student B
You are angry with your partner. Tell her/him what she/he said earlier, and what she/he did. Talk about other things she/he has done wrong!	Explain what happened, and give good reasons for what you did. Add comments about what your partner said earlier.

3 What do you think it is like to be famous? What problems do famous people have with their families?

Compare the magazine texts. What differences are there?

BELLA AND THE BUTLER – *The True Story*

Norman Harris, once the butler at Hollywood star Bella Brown's luxury home, talked to *Starlight's* Jean Forsyth.

1 'Don't believe everything you see in the cinema,' said Norman Harris, as he told me about the two years he spent looking after glamour star Bella Brown
5 and her family. 'They say she's the perfect mother, but half the time she was never at home. And I ought to know. I only left because I felt so sorry for the rest of the family.'
10 According to Norman, Bella's mother, 1930s singing star Loulou Campbell, spends all the time arguing with Sam Pocket, who is Bella's husband number five. 'In fact, Sam has moved out of the
15 house,' Norman revealed. 'Bella is going to divorce him because she wants to marry someone else.' The someone else, says Norman, is Wall Street banker Harvey D. Greenbag. 'He spends most
20 of his time in Bella's house already,' Norman added. 'And the children treated me as a slave.' Bella's son Jackson, 18, invited all his friends for all-night parties by the swimming
25 pool. 'I had to run after them. And Suzanne, the daughter, keeps a tiger in her bedroom. I hate animals.'

BUTLER AND FRIEND To the Stars

Here in London interviews the perfect gentleman's (and lady's) gentleman.

1 There is something special about Norman Harris. 'More than a butler' as Bella Brown put it, 'more of a friend.' After eighteen months in Miss
5 Brown's Hollywood home, Norman Harris is the man that all the stars are talking about. 'I am sorry I came home, of course,' Norman told me, as he showed me the many photographs
10 which still remind him of his happy months in California. 'Miss Brown is a perfect mother, working for her was a pleasure. I asked Norman about the rest of the family. Was it
15 true that Bella's children call him "Uncle Norman"? 'They are wonderful children, both of them.' Did he have a favourite, I asked? 'Well, Miss Suzanne and I both love animals. She
20 has some lovely pets. And young Jackson was always kind to me.' I asked him about Bella's husband, Sam. 'They make a perfect couple,' said Norman, 'and Mr Pocket often
25 spends the evening playing the piano, and Mrs Campbell, Bella's mother, sings. It's a lovely family. But they are travelling round the world together at the moment, so I decided to come
30 home.'

What did Norman tell *Starlight* magazine, and what did he tell *Here In London* magazine? Add six more differences.

He told 'Starlight' that Bella Brown was never at home, but he told 'Here in London' that she was a perfect mother.

Pre-reading

1 What are the differences between people of these ages: 10, 16, 25, 40? Discuss them using these topics:

clothes   friends   habits   interests   family relations

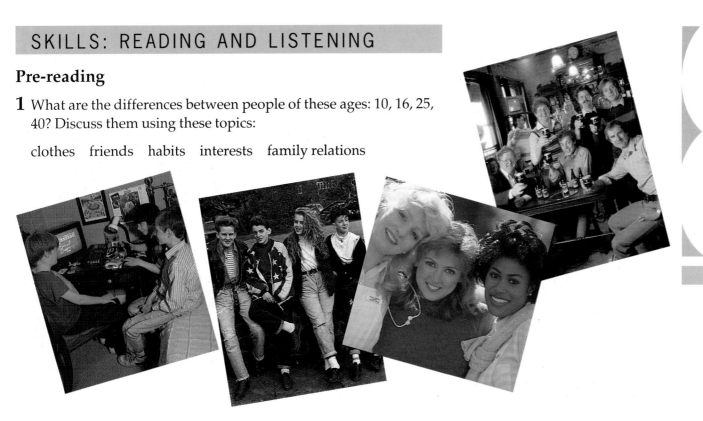

Reading

2 Read quickly through the text and decide whether it was written by a parent, a teenager, or neither.

Rebels without a pause

1 Parents should stop blaming themselves. I've come to the conclusion there's not a lot you can do about it.

I mean the teenage years. Whatever you do or
5 however you choose to handle it, at some point between the ages of 12 and 18 that wonderful, reasonable and helpful child will turn into a snarling, loutish monster.

I've seen friends handle it in all kinds of different
10 ways. One is a strict disciplinarian and insisted her son, right from a small child, should stand up whenever anyone entered the room, open doors, shake hands and generally behave as the model son. I saw him last week when I called round. Stretched
15 full length on the sofa, he made no attempt to turn off the lurid video he was watching as I walked in, and his greeting was no more than a grunt.

His mother was mortified. 'I don't know what to do with him these days,' she said. 'He's forgotten all
20 the manners we taught him.'

He hasn't forgotten them. He's just decided that he's not going to use them.

It's getting her down though, and she confessed that she had actually come up behind him and tried to
25 heave the sofa over to tip him off. The things parents go through!

Another chum let her daughters climb all over the furniture, reach across the table, stare at you and say, 'I don't like your frock, it's smelly.'
30 One of the same daughters has recently been expelled from school. The other has left home with a lad who arrived one night, dressed in black leather, on a motorbike, taking her and all her worldly goods on the pillion.
35 'Where did we go wrong?' her parents now sob. Probably nowhere much. At least, no more than the rest of that unfortunate race, parents.

Comprehension check

3 How much can you remember without looking at the text?

a How did the friend's son use to behave when he was a child?

b How does he behave now?

c How did the other friend's daughters behave when they were young?

Word search

4 a What is the difference between: *a snarling, loutish monster* or *a wonderful, reasonable and helpful child*? Which verb describes the 'change'?

b Does a *strict disciplinarian* let children do whatever they want?

5 Decide what these words and phrases mean.

a *lurid* What kind of video do you think he was watching?

b *grunt* Which animal sounds like this?

c *mortified* How do you think his mother felt? The cartoon helps.

d *'I don't like your frock, it's smelly'*. Is this polite or not?

e *expelled* Is this something good or bad? Guess what happened.

f *pillion* Where was she sitting on the motorbike?

Reading

6 Read the rest of the text and decide whether these statements say the same as the text.

a The writer told her mother not to give her son any more earrings.

b Why can't my mother say that he looks stupid if she wants to?

c Teenagers seem to think that parents are stupid.

d Mothers who are smokers notice when their children smoke.

e Parents do not like it when their children lie to them.

> 1 Why do we always blame ourselves for the teenage years of our children? Why do we keep being patient with someone who has now become as reasonable and charming as a maddened gorilla?
>
> 'Don't have a go at him about the earring,' I said to my mother, when my son
> 5 suddenly appeared with a pierced ear one Saturday.
>
> But why shouldn't she mention she thinks he looks a complete banana if she wants to? There we are treating them gently just to keep the peace, when they're being about as careful not to hurt our feelings as a herd of mad elephants.
>
> What's hardest of all is suddenly not getting on with this person whom we've
> 10 always liked and been proud of. One of their many annoying teenage traits is that they appear to think parents have lost all their senses, intelligence and powers of deduction.
>
> For instance, cigarette smoke is pretty noticeable if you don't smoke yourself. So you go up to your child's bedroom and say, conversationally and trying to keep it
> 15 low key, 'So when did you start smoking?'
>
> The reply, when it comes, is an insult not only to your intelligence, but also to your sense of smell. 'I don't smoke, Mum.' That's when most mothers, quite rightly, lose their temper. It might help just a little if teenagers could learn that what annoys a parent more than anything is lying about an obvious fact. But no
> 20 doubt they'll continue to think that parents they've looked up to have become dull, stupid and not worth a civil word. That's the trouble with parents, most teenagers will tell you: they go through this really awful stage when you've got nothing in common with them. It's not true, of course. It's just that during their teenage years, my children just don't understand me.

Listening

7 🎧 Listen to an interview describing what a mother, a father and their sons said about family life. For each statement, complete what the person interviewed actually said.

She didn't know why her children had changed.
'I don't know why my children have changed.'

a 'I have ...

b 'They do ...

c 'My sons have ...

d 'I wasn't ...

e 'I decided that ...

f 'When we go ...

What do you think about the relationships between the members of this family? Do you approve of their behaviour?

Speaking

8 What complaints might a teenager have about his or her parents? Do teenagers have the same problems in your country?

GRAMMAR PRACTICE

Reported statements ▶ 7.1

1 Match each sentence in Direct Speech with the same sentence written as Reported Speech. <u>Underline</u> all the changes.

'I'll be home late tonight. Don't bother to wait up.'
He said he <u>would</u> be home late and <u>told them not</u> to wait up.

a 'You went out late last night.'
b 'I'm meeting some friends at the pub.'
c 'But you haven't done all your homework yet.'
d 'I'm going to finish it tomorrow morning when I get up.'
e 'You won't have enough time in the morning.'
f 'I'll have plenty of time because I don't have to go to college.'
g 'Don't make a lot of noise when you come in.'

1 He said he was meeting some friends at the pub.
2 He said he was going to finish it the next morning when he got up.
3 They told him not to make a lot of noise when he came in.
4 They said that he hadn't done all his homework.
5 They told him that he wouldn't have enough time the next morning.
6 He said he would have plenty of time because he didn't have to go to college.
7 They said he had been out late the night before.

2 What were the actual words that the people said in the statements below?

His mother said that he didn't understand her problems.
'You don't understand my problems.'

a Her grandmother said that all young people were lazy and unreliable.
b His mother said he would go crazy if he listened to music all day.
c She told her father that he was too old-fashioned to understand her.
d His parents told him that he hadn't treated them very well.
e He told his sister that people kept telling him what to do.
f His grandmother told him that his parents were too easy-going.
g She said that her mother expected her to do the housework.
h Their father told them that he expected them to be home by 10.30.
i His parents told him that they wanted him to have all the things they hadn't had.
j He told his mother that her ideas were out of date.

3 Report these statements.

'Young people complain too much about their parents.'
He said young people complained too much about their parents.

a 'An elder brother or sister is always helpful.'
b 'Most young people will think differently when they get older.'
c 'Young people have become the most important part of society.'
d 'Most older people are living in a world they don't understand.'
e 'The problem of the old is becoming more serious all the time.'
f 'Families which discuss their problems are happy families.'
g 'Many children don't realise that they have upset their parents.'
h 'Large families usually have fewer problems.'
i 'An only child has more advantages than a child from a large family.'
j 'A family which plays together, stays together.'

Time and other changes in reported speech ► 7.1

4 Rewrite each sentence as direct speech.

  a Keith told Freddy he would see him the next day.
  b George told Peter to put his (Peter's) bag in his (George's) room.
  c Martin told Julie that he had seen her brother the day before.
  d Sally told Dave that his letters were on her desk.
  e Trevor told Mandy that the money was hers.
  f Harry told Sue and Jean that he was going to miss them.

5 Rewrite each sentence as reported speech.

  a 'Paul, post this letter tomorrow,' said Brenda.
  b 'The large brown bag is mine,' said Jack.
  c 'I'll be here tomorrow,' said Shirley.
  d 'Mary, these books are yours,' said Harry.
  e 'There was an accident opposite my house yesterday,' said Jane.
  f 'I haven't been here before,' said Brian.

Ask and *tell* ► 7.3

6 Match each sentence in direct speech with the sentence which reports it.

'Do you think you could close the door please?'
He asked me to close the door.

  a 'Do you think you could open the window please?'
  b 'Give me the money, now!'
  c 'Could you possibly carry this bag for me?'
  d 'Hey you, carry this bag.'
  e 'Could you give me that money, please?'
  f 'Open the window, quick!'

  1 She asked me to carry the bag.
  2 He told me to open the window.
  3 She told me to give her the money.
  4 He asked me to open the window.
  5 She asked me to give her the money.
  6 He told me to carry the bag.

Say and *tell* ► 7.3

7 For each sentence, put *told* or *said* into the space.

  a Jack _____ his parents he was going to a party.
  b He _____ them not to worry.
  c His mother _____ him to phone her from the party.
  d He _____ his friends would think he was being silly.
  e His father _____ his mother would worry unless he phoned.
  f He _____ his parents he would do it if he remembered.
  g His mother _____ him to promise to phone.
  h He _____ he was no longer a child and started to leave.
  i His father _____ him he couldn't have the car after all.
  j Jack _____ he didn't care, and left.

SKILLS: LISTENING AND WRITING

Pre-listening

1 Study the family tree of characters from *The Wilbies*, a TV soap opera. Decide who said each statement. What do you think the story is about?

THE WILBIES

Jake Wilbie = Laura Wilbie

Luke Wilbie = Kathy   Marilyn Wilbie = Bill

- **a** 'I can't believe that such a terrible thing has happened. And I'm sure that no one in the family has done anything wrong.'
- **b** Mother and Father need my help. I have to keep the family and the company together.'
- **c** 'I'm going to take everything that's mine. You think you're clever, but I've always been better than you!'
- **d** 'I fought for what I've got, and no one is going to take it away. It is mine by right!'
- **e** 'I haven't been in the family long, but I already hate them all. They all tell me what to do. I am not a child!'

Listening

2 Listen to characters from *The Wilbies* talking about the family. Decide who is speaking and who they are talking about.

3 Study the statements below. Are these accurate reports of what you heard on the cassette? Rewrite any inaccurate sentences.

- **a** Luke said he knew that Jake had murdered the dead man.
- **b** Marilyn said that the house and the oil company belonged to Kathy.
- **c** Kathy said that the police knew her father was lying.
- **d** Jake said that he had done something wrong but no one knew it.
- **e** Laura said her husband had been out on the night of the murder.

Writing

4 Rewrite this scene from *The Wilbies* as dialogue. Begin:

Detective: Where were you . . .

First the detective asked Jake where he had been on the night of the murder. He said that he had been working at his office. The detective told him that Laura had said that he had been at the house with her. Jake said that she had been trying to help him. Then he said that he had not killed his son-in-law. He said that Kathy had been talking with him at the office that night. He said that Kathy wanted a divorce from Luke. Kathy said that it was true. Then the detective asked Luke where he had been that night. He said that he couldn't remember. Then Marilyn said that on the night her husband had been murdered, she had met Luke for a drink in a bar near Jake's office. The detective asked her about the time. She said it had been at about nine. Then he asked Luke what they had talked about. Luke said they had talked about Bill. He said that Marilyn had wanted to be head of the oil company instead of her husband.

5 Who killed Bill? Discuss these points.

motive: why?
method: how?
events: what happened?

Write the murderer's confession, beginning:
It's true, I killed him...

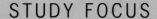

STUDY FOCUS

Check your grammar

Reported speech: paraphrasing

1 Reporting what people say usually involves paraphrasing as it is often unnecessary (and uninteresting) to report every word. Study the sentences below and try to report them in the number of words given.

  a 'To be quite honest, I'm not the slightest bit interested in antique furniture.'
    She said she .... (6 words)

  b 'Yes, of course you can borrow my car, any time you like.'
    He said I .... (4 words)

  c 'Put that box on the table, you stupid idiot!'
    She told me .... (7 words)

  d 'You look really awful, go and brush your hair.'
    She told me to ....(3 words)

Reported speech: without back-shift

2 These reports do **not** follow the rules for tense changes (back-shift). Decide why it is not necessary to change the verbs underlined.

Look, Gerry said *he's leaving* in five minutes and *he'll meet* us at the pub round the corner.'

As the words were spoken very recently, the speaker feels that the actions (*is leaving*, *will meet*) are still 'present'.

  a The programme said that the planets *are moving* nearer to the sun.
  b He told me that he *wants* to marry me.
  c He told me what this word *means*.
  d Our teacher said that we *are making* good progress.

Build your vocabulary

Character and feelings

1 Study the list of words describing character and feelings. Divide the list into positive (+) words and negative (–) words.

old-fashioned	shy	lonely	helpful
strict	annoying	honest	jealous
reliable	lazy	easy-going	understanding

2 Add other similar words that you know to your lists.

Practise your pronunciation

Unstressed syllables

1 a ▥ Listen and repeat the words from the list.

fashionable	reliable
miserable	enjoyable
adaptable	valuable
understandable	acceptable

  b Mark the main stress in each word by (circling) the stressed syllable. Is there a rule about the pronunciation of the *-able* ending? Is it pronounced like *table*? Check the pronunciation of the symbol /ə/ (schwa).

2 ▥ Listen and repeat the words from the list. What is the sound **in bold**? Is it a stressed sound?

to**ma**to	quar**re**l
about	**pic**ture
for**ge**t	mod**er**n
fa**the**r	fash**io**n
lem**o**n	tra**ve**l

72

Unit 9 All in the mind

Different lifestyles

1 Would you like to be one of these people? How would you spend your time? What would you do?

2 On a piece of paper, write the name of a famous person who is living now. Exchange pieces of paper.

Imagine your life as the person named on the piece of paper you receive. Describe how you would live and what you would do. Others have to guess who you are.

LANGUAGE ACTIVITIES

▶ Conditional 1: real situations
▶ Conditional 2: imaginary situations

1 How good are you at solving puzzles? You go to visit some friends, and you find this note on the door of the flat. What is the explanation?

Just then one of your friends arrives and explains everything. The pictures show what he says. Continue his explanation by making five more statements beginning: *'If . . .*

If you ring the doorbell, the dog will bark.

> Don't ring the doorbell - or I'll have to ring for a pizza.
>
> Julie

Conditional 1: real situations   5.1

If you ring the doorbell, the dog **will bark**.
If you knock quietly the dog **won't bark**.

1 2 3 4 5

6

7

2 Comment on the situation of your friends, the dog and the baby. Think of four more things to say.

If you write mysterious notes like this one, nobody will understand.

3 You like telling your friends what to do! This picture shows their flat. Make some comments beginning: *If . . .*

If you play with the baby more, it'll stop crying.

4 Do you ever imagine changing the way you live? What do you think the people shown above would like to change?

What do you think these people are day-dreaming about? Make a statement for each person beginning: *If . . .*

Conditional 2: imaginary situations   5.2

If I had a car, *I would (I'd)* drive to work.
If I were rich, *I could* give up work completely!
If I worked nearer home, *I'd have* more free time.

Write a few words on a piece of paper to describe your day-dream. Give it to a partner. Make some statements about the day-dreams of the person who gave you the piece of paper.

5 Look at the pictures. What do you think these people are saying? What advice are they giving? Say their words.

Giving advice   8.2

If *I were you, I'd* turn left.
It *might be better if* you took that road.

Role play

6 Practise giving advice using one of the situations shown in question 5. Try to find a practical solution!

Student A
You want some advice, but you find it difficult to accept the advice that others give you. Describe your problem. Give as many details as possible. Ask for some advice, and explain what you think about the advice you receive.

Student B
Give some advice for the situation. Try to be sympathetic and practical. Offer a variety of different solutions.

SKILLS: READING AND LISTENING

Pre-reading

1 Read this letter written to a magazine Problem Page.

> ### FAILURE
>
> I am only twenty-two, but I already feel as if I am a complete failure! People seem to ignore me or just push me around, I have no friends, and I worry all the time. I just don't seem to have any confidence. I feel tired all the time, though my doctor says there is nothing the matter with me. What do you think I should do?

What advice would you give? Use the topics in the list.

looks	work	family	friends
activities	behaviour	feelings	the future

Reading

2 Read through the article and decide whether the advice given is the same as the advice you discussed in question 1. Underline a sentence in each section which gives the most important, or most general, advice.

CREATE A NEW, SELF-CONFIDENT YOU!

1 Communication
Your thoughts and feelings are important, so communicating them is vital. You're more likely to get what you want if you can ask in a direct, open way. Even if you don't get your way, you'll feel stronger in yourself as a result. Increase your communication skills by writing down your views and desires. Say them to yourself in a mirror or record them on cassette. By practising like this you'll feel less nervous when you really do have to speak up. Learn to voice your feelings – no one else will do it for you.

2 Body Language
The way we use our bodies conveys even more about our feelings than the things we say. Think how you use your body when talking. Direct eye contact, upright posture, emphasising gestures and a lively tone of voice are signs of assertiveness. Looking away from people, crossing your arms and fidgeting are signs which say your self-esteem is low. Observe others and think what your body's saying.

3 Think Positive!
Sufferers of low self-esteem tend to have negative thoughts about themselves: 'I'm a failure, I am boring...' and so on. If you don't respect yourself, how can you expect others to respect you? So concentrate on your positive traits and write them down. They may not be earth-shattering – maybe you're a sympathetic listener, or a caring parent. Ask a close friend or relative to list your pluses. The two lists could well reveal bonuses you never knew you had.

4 Taking the Blame
Constantly taking the blame when things go wrong is a sign of low self-esteem. We all make mistakes. But if you're for ever saying: 'It's my fault,' or 'I shouldn't have said it,' and 'I've done it again,' you'll end up self-conscious and embarrassed and self-esteem will plummet, leaving you afraid to assert yourself. If you've blundered, admit it. But remember, one blunder doesn't make you a blunderer for ever. Learn from your mistake and avoid it next time.

5 Enthusiasm
Remember how you feel when you're doing something you feel strongly about. It's impossible to feel bad about yourself at such moments. Think what you feel most strongly about and develop these things into as many interests as possible. Maybe you could join a social, political or campaign organisation – how about drama, a competitive sport or an absorbing hobby?

6 Winning Targets
Life's winners set themselves targets they know for sure they can reach. Losers set themselves impossible goals and thus their low self-esteem is confirmed when they inevitably fail. So set yourself realistic goals. For example, if you feel the need to diet, don't aim to lose ten kilos in two weeks. Instead, try for an attainable loss – say one kilo in a week. Winners recognise that each step towards a goal is a success in itself. And, there's nothing like success for boosting the ego.

7 Pamper Yourself
Give yourself regular treats, as if you're spoiling someone you love. Buy that special outfit, go for a slap-up meal, award yourself a day in bed with a good book – anything which makes you feel good. If you can indulge others, you can indulge yourself. It'll give you a warm glow – and boost that self esteem.

Comprehension check

3 Decide whether the advice below is given in the article.

Paragraph:

1 Say what you want as clearly as possible.
2 Don't look people in the eye too much when you talk to them.
3 Make a note of all your faults.
4 Don't blame yourself for everything.
5 Try not to feel bad about yourself when you do sports or hobbies.
6 Don't give yourself impossible tasks to do.
7 Try to read more and go to bed early.

Word search

4 Find phrases in the article which could be replaced by:

a It's very important to say what you think or feel.
b You have to teach yourself how to put your feelings into words.
c Ways of showing that you are expressing yourself confidently.
d Think more about the good sides of your character.
e If you can be good to other people, be good to yourself too.

5 Find words or phrases in the text which could be replaced by:

Paragraph 1
very important
it's more probable that you'll
strong wishes
anxious or worried

Paragraph 2
shows
position of standing up straight
moving nervously
carefully watch

Paragraph 3
amazingly good
someone good at listening to others
show very good points

Paragraph 4
fall to a low level

Paragraph 6
making yourself feel better

Paragraph 7
set of clothes

Pre-listening

6 If you had these problems, what could you do to improve the situation?

you are shy
you feel nervous and worried
you feel bored
you are always tired
you are aggressive and noisy
you tell lies
you lack confidence
you laugh too much
you are lonely

Listening

7 ⌷ Listen to people describing problems they used to have. Write two words which describe each person's problem.

PROBLEMS			
Angela	**Nick**	**David**	**Marion**
shy			

8 ⌷ Can you remember how each person solved their problems? Before you listen again, discuss what you can remember. Listen again and make notes about the solutions.

SOLUTIONS			
Angela	**Nick**	**David**	**Marion**
She joined a drama group, and met more people.			

GRAMMAR PRACTICE

Conditionals 1 and 2 ▶ 5.1, 5.2

1 Study the part sentences below. Label each one conditional 1 or 2. Complete the sentences in a way that makes sense.

   a If I saw a dangerous snake, I . . .
   b If I have any free time later, I . . .
   c If you phone me tomorrow, . . .
   d If I won some money, I . . .
   e If I told you what I think, . . .
   f If you let me copy your homework, I . . .
   g If you need any money, I . . .
   h If I were alone in a large old house, I . . .
   i If you keep annoying me, I . . .
   j If someone pushed me on the bus, I . . .

2 Study each sentence and decide whether it is a conditional 1 or 2 sentence. Then answer the question that follows.

   a *If a famous pop star talked to me I wouldn't know what to say.*
     Am I at a party with a lot of famous pop stars in the room?
   b *If I knew the answer to the question, I'd tell you.*
     Do you know the answer?
   c *If you get into difficulties, I'll come and give you a hand.*
     Am I offering to help you?
   d *If you fell in the water, I would rescue you.*
     Do I think you are going to fall in?
   e *If I had a thousand pounds, I wouldn't give you a penny!*
     Am I expecting to get a lot of money from somewhere?

3 Choose words from the list below to describe the kind of character in each sentence in question 2.

honest	aggressive	kind
dishonest	nervous	mean
friendly	shy	generous
selfish	brave	reliable
bad-tempered	rude	helpful

Conditional 2: imaginary situations ▶ 5.2

4 Answer these questions.

   a What would an honest person do if they found a wallet in the street?
   b What would a generous person do if they had a lot of money?
   c What would a selfish person do if they were in a dangerous situation?
   d What would a rude person do if they were getting on a bus?
   e What would a reliable person do if they arranged to meet you?
   f What would a nervous person do before an important examination?
   g What would an aggressive person do if you stepped on their foot?
   h What would a dishonest person do if you left them alone in your house?
   i What would a helpful person do if you were lost?
   j What would a brave person do if the school caught fire?

Real and imaginary situations: conditional 1 and conditional 2

5 Study the situations and complete the statement after each one.

You park your car outside someone's driveway so they cannot move their car. An angry person comes from the house and says:
If you don't move your car, I'll call the police.

a You are trying to climb in through the second floor window of your house after forgetting your keys. A neighbour watching you says:
If I had a . . .

b You have no money left this week. You phone a friend and say:
If you . . .

c You are about to go out for a walk. It looks as if it might rain. Someone offers you an umbrella and says:
If you don't . . .

d You are always late for work. Your boss calls you into his office and says:
You wouldn't . . .

e You never have any breakfast. Every morning you feel hungry by 10.30. A friend says:
You wouldn't . . .

f Your train leaves at 6.00. You arrive at the station at 5.58. You start running and say to your friend:
If we . . .

Giving advice ▶ 8.2

6 Give some advice to the people with the problems described below, using the forms given in the example.

I feel tired all the time, and never go out or do anything interesting. I am eighteen years old.

If I were you, I'd take more exercise and make some friends.
If you did more you wouldn't feel so tired. I think you should take up a hobby or something like that.

a I never have any money. I don't know why. And I'm always in debt.

b I'd like to go abroad for a holiday, but I'm scared. I can't speak any foreign languages, and I don't really know where to go.

c I have a lot of problems with my neighbours. They are very noisy, and their garden is full of rubbish. I want to remain friends but . . .

d I have a problem with my dog. When people come to the house, it barks a lot, and frightens them.

e I have just won £100,000 on the football pools. The problem is that I'm not sure what to do with it. I don't want to waste it on silly things.

f I feel tired all the time, and seem to catch a lot of colds, and generally get ill. What would you advise?

g I just can't seem to be able to write anything when I have to write a composition in English. Do you have any advice?

h I am a very popular singer (I'm not going to tell you my name!). My problem is that people follow me everywhere, and I keep getting offers of marriage. Help me please!

Listening

1 ☒ Study this advertisement from a magazine. Listen to extracts of what people can hear when they phone these numbers. For each extract, decide which number you are listening to.

Exams – How to Get Through	**0889 5551**
Pen-pals Make New Friends	**0889 6062**
Vanessa King She Answers Your Problems	**0889 6061**
How to Make Him Notice You	**0889 8882**
I Don't Get On With My Parents	**0889 3032**

Pre-writing

2 Read this letter which was sent to a magazine problem page. Read the reply given.

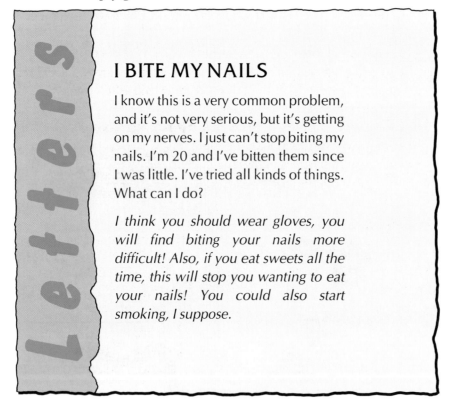

I BITE MY NAILS

I know this is a very common problem, and it's not very serious, but it's getting on my nerves. I just can't stop biting my nails. I'm 20 and I've bitten them since I was little. I've tried all kinds of things. What can I do?

I think you should wear gloves, you will find biting your nails more difficult! Also, if you eat sweets all the time, this will stop you wanting to eat your nails! You could also start smoking, I suppose.

Do you think this is good advice? What would you write?

3 What problems do people usually write to magazines about? Add four more problems to this list.

appearance   travel   driving   money

Writing

4 Choose one of the problems you have discussed and plan a short letter to a magazine describing the problem, and asking for advice. Choose points from the list below.

Describe what you or someone else:

always do
did or didn't do
would do if . . .
have always done
told someone
are doing now
want to do

5 When you have written your letter, seal it in an envelope and write this address on the front. How will you set out the address on the envelope?

**Twenties Magazine,
Vanessa King,
London,
40 Norwich Road,
W2Q 8MC**

Deliver the letters around the class so that everyone receives a problem. Read the letter you receive, and decide what advice to give.

Write your reply and send it back to the person who wrote it.

Have you received good advice?

Check your grammar

If ... sentences

1 Study these *If ...* sentences, and label the ones which follow the patterns conditional 1 or 2. Not all *If ...* sentences are conditional sentences.

   a If you ask her, she always says no.
   b If I had the money, I'd buy a new washing machine.
   c If you didn't like the taste, why did you eat it?
   d If you leave now, you'll catch the bus easily.
   e If I were you, I wouldn't sit by the window.
   f If it was too cold for swimming, we played football on the beach.

2 Can any of the sentences **a** to **f** be rewritten without *if* and with *when* or *so*?

Build your vocabulary

Explaining words

1 Use a dictionary to complete the explanations of the words underlined which are all connected with the topic of **money**.

   a If you have a <u>debt</u> ....
   b People usually <u>earn</u> ....
   c A <u>fare</u> is what you pay ....
   d If you are <u>generous</u> ....
   e If you are <u>mean</u> ....
   f It is possible to <u>win</u> ....

2 Write similar explanations for these words which are connected with the topic of **money**.

bill	economical	owe	value
cash	fee	purchase	wallet

Practise your pronunciation

Unstressed syllables

1 How would you pronounce the words in the list? Where does the main stress fall? Which syllables have a /ə/ (schwa) sound?

   a helpful
      careful
      beautiful
      successful
      cheerful

   b generous
      courageous
      adventurous
      jealous
      luxurious

   🔊 Listen and repeat the list. Were you right?

Sentence stress

2 🔊 Listen and repeat these sentences. <u>Underline</u> the words which have most stress.

   a If I were you, I'd go by bus.
   b I wouldn't do that if I were you.
   c If I were you, I'd stay at home.
   d If I were you, I'd take an aspirin.
   e I wouldn't tell her if I were you.

Unit 10 Just good friends

Telling the story

1 What happened in the picture story? Tell your version of the story.

2 What is missing from the speech bubbles?

3 What do you think are the main problems in this story? Who is to blame? What did the characters do wrong?

LANGUAGE ACTIVITIES

▶ Describing people
▶ Introductions
▶ Reported questions

1 How long have you known your friends? What do you talk about? How often do you see them? What makes a good friend? Add four more points to the ones below.

> **A Friend Is Someone Who . . .**
> *you like a lot*
> *helps you*

> **Relative clauses 11**
>
> **Subject clauses**
>
> *A friend is someone who helps you.*
>
> **Object clauses**
>
> *A friend is someone (who) you like a lot.*

1

2

3

2 Do your friends sometimes annoy you? How would you feel in these situations?

1

2

What annoys you, and what doesn't annoy you about people? Think about friends, colleagues at work, and people you meet. Think of four positive and four negative points for these situations.

at parties	on your birthday	on public transport
at work	in emergencies	on holiday

What sort of people do you like? Use the same situations to describe them.

It really annoys me when someone pushes in front of me in a queue.

People who smoke at work really annoy me.

3

3 If you met someone for the first time, what would you ask them?

You are at a party, and meet people for the first time. What would you say to someone who asked you:

how much you earned?	if you were married?
what your phone number was?	if you had a car?
where you came from?	if you wanted a cigarette?
how much you paid for your coat?	if you had a sister?

Make a list of five questions which are suitable for a first meeting. Report the questions to a partner.

4 What do you think the people in the pictures are saying?

Which people in the pictures could begin like this:

Can I ...	*Can you ...*	*Could I ...*
Could you ...	*Would you ...*	

What would you say in these situations to someone you do not know very well?

a The other person looks ill. Offer him an aspirin.
b Your car has broken down. Ask someone to push it.
c You have just met an interesting person. Invite him/her to lunch at your house on Sunday.
d Some new neighbours are moving in. Offer to help.

Role play

5

Student A	Student B
You are at a party. You are a very shy person. You have just met your partner for the first time. He/She talks to you but you find it difficult to answer his/her questions.	You are at a party. You have just met your partner for the first time. You like asking a lot of questions. Try to find out as much as possible about him/her.

6 Report the conversation to a different partner. Decide if this was a successful first meeting.

Indirect and reported questions   7.2

Direct question

'How much do you earn?'
'Are you married'

Indirect question

I would ask her **how much she earned**.
I would ask him **if he was married**.

Reported question

He asked me **how much I earned**.
She asked me **if I was married**.

Pre-reading

1 These situations describe ways in which a couple might meet. Which ones do you think are most common, and which ones most unusual?

at work, school   a computer dating agency
on a train, bus   an arrangement by parents
an advertisement   at a disco

Reading

2 How many points which you discussed in question 1 are mentioned in the text?

Couples ... BY COMPUTER

1 Jenny Taylor stood before the altar and turned to look into the loving eyes of her bridegroom Robert Ben-
nett. A perfect couple. Anyone in the
5 congregation last Easter Saturday would have agreed. But few of them realised this match wasn't made in heaven. It was made by machine, not Cupid. A dating agency computer
10 had brought them together. And Jenny and Robert are far from unique. A staggering one in every *five* of Britain's ten million single people have used a dating agency.

15 Psychologist Dr Alan Drummond, who has made a four-year study on blind dates, estimates that more than 30,000 of them take place each week. 'The most important rea-
20 son for the boom in the romance industry is the high divorce rate for people in their thirties and forties,' he explains. 'They find themselves single once again, but have
25 lost most of their single friends.'

Lisa, 44, and Simon, 43, always tell people they met at a party. In fact they met via a dating agency. Both are teachers who moved to the
30 Midlands to work. They have been together for three years. It was Lisa who insisted on the secrecy. 'I don't think people at school would have been intentionally cruel, but there
35 would have been a lot of leg-pulling,' she says. Lisa and Simon plan to marry later this year. Simon wanted to get married within months of their first meeting, but Lisa preferred to
40 wait. 'I'd answered advertisements and joined agencies on and off for six years. In that time your confidence goes right up and right down,' she explains. 'I suppose I did feel a
45 bit of social reject. But I was determined not just to settle for anybody.

Then I found Simon.'

Rosalyn Townsend doesn't give up so easily either. A glamorous
50 32-year-old, she has spent three years and a small fortune searching the small ads for a good-looking, wealthy husband. Now, 700 letters later, Rosalyn is still placing and
55 replying to ads. Three-times divorced Rosalyn says finding a father for her three-year-old daughter Lucy is her prime concern. Including the cost of travel and posh frocks to
60 wear to her dates, the bill for her man-hunt adds up to £10,000!

Comprehension check

3 Answer these questions, using your own words as far as possible.

a Why do so many people use dating agencies, according to Dr Drummond?

b Why did Lisa and Simon keep their use of the agency a secret?

c What exactly has Rosalyn spent £10,000 on?

Word search

4 Decide what these words from the text mean. For each word choose from the possible explanations given.

a *altar*: kind of photographer / part of church

b *congregation*: people in church / large family party

c *match*: joining of two people / marriage in church

d *unique*: the only one / unhappy in love

e *staggering*: lonely and unhappy / very surprising

Comprehension check

5 Are these statements **true** (t) or **false** (f) according to the text?

a Two million single people in Britain have used a dating agency.

b More than 30,000 studies of blind dates have been made.

c Many people who use dating agencies have been married before.

d It took Lisa about three years before she found Simon.

e Rosalyn Townsend has spent £10,000 on computer dating agencies.

Word search

6 Find words or phrases in the text that could be replaced by:

sudden increase
not wanted by society
rich
on purpose
finally choose

main interest
making jokes
very attractive
expensive dresses

Speaking

7 Did you find anything in the text which surprised you? Would this way of meeting people be successful in your country?

Listening

8 Tell the story in the cartoon.

Listen to four people talking about going on a date. Which speaker on the cassette is telling the story in the cartoon?

Which is the best description of the cartoon?

a When you are on a romantic date, your friends often make fun of you.

b Girls and boys have different ideas of a romantic evening.

c Boys behave in a different way when they are with their male friends.

d Most people talk in a strange way when they are with their friends.

Speaking

9 Do you think that the way people behave depends on who they are with?

Reported questions ▶ 7.2

1 Write each reported question as a direct question.

He asked me if I knew his brother.
Do you know my brother?

a He wanted to know if I had met his sister.
b She asked me why I had left my children at home.
c He asked me what time I was going home.
d I asked her if she had seen any good films recently.
e She asked me where I had been working last year.
f He asked me if I lived with my parents.

Reporting verbs ▶ 7.3

2 Write each direct question as a reported question.

'How old are you, John?' asked Jean.
Jean asked John how old he was.

a 'What's the time, Peter?' asked Jack.
b 'Are you enjoying yourself, Wendy?' asked Denis.
c 'When are we going to have dinner, Richard?' asked Martin.
d 'Did you come to my last party, Bill?' asked Irene.
e 'Why do you keep staring at me, Jane?' asked Michael.
f 'Is it time to go home yet, Mary?' asked Chris.

Reported speech ▶ 7

3 Match the sentences with the reports which paraphrase what was said.

'I don't care, I won't go.'
Peter refused to go.

a 'I don't care, I won't go.'
b 'Would you like a drink?'
c 'Oh dear, I'm terribly sorry.'
d 'Stella, this is my brother Peter.'
e 'She smokes all the time!'
f 'No thanks.'
g 'Can I give you a lift home?'
h 'Karen, have you met Cathy?'
i 'These buses never come.'
j 'Sorry about last night.'
k 'Need some help?'
l 'Sorry, I'm too busy.'

1 Peter refused to go.
2 Peter complained about the buses.
3 Cathy refused a cigarette.
4 Peter offered her a lift.
5 Cathy offered him a drink.
6 Peter introduced her to his sister.
7 Sue introduced her to her brother.
8 Karen apologised.
9 Sue refused to help.
10 Karen complained about her.
11 Peter apologised for this behaviour.
12 Cathy offered to help him.

87

Relative clauses: object ▶ 11

4 Join each pair of sentences using *who* and making necessary changes.

Stella is a girl, I sat next to her at her school.
*Stella is **a** girl (who) I sat next to at school.* (one of many)
*Stella is **the** girl (who) I sat next to at school.* (the only one)

a Bill is a teacher. I met him in Athens.
b Christine is a girl. I lived next door to her once.
c Tom is a friend. I went on holiday with him last year.
d Helen is a tall girl. You met her yesterday.
e John is a friend. I stayed with him in London.
f Jane is a talkative person. You asked her to tell you about the film.
g Peter is a bearded man. I introduced him to you earlier.
h Jenny is a girl. I bought my car from her.
i Chris is a friend. I copy my homework from him.
j Mary is a girl. Everyone really likes her.

Relative clauses: subject ▶ 11

5 Rewrite each pair of sentences to make a sentence like the one below.

Some people always smile. I like this.
I like people who always smile.

a Some people talk too much. I don't like this.
b Some people have interesting things to say. I like this.
c Some people say nice things about me. I love this.
d Some people know how to enjoy themselves. I like this.
e Some people cause trouble. I don't like this.
f Some people share everything with others. I like this.
g Some people make me laugh. I love this.
h Some people don't return what I lend them. I don't like this.
i Some people think they know everything. I don't like this.
j Some people try to be friends with everyone. I like this.

Relative clauses: subject and object ▶ 11

6 Check that you understand the difference between the different types of relative clauses in question 4 and question 6. Complete each sentence. Leave out the relative *who* where possible.

I met that girl yesterday.
That's the girl ...
That's the girl I met yesterday.

a That man used to live near here.
That's the man ...
b That girl passed the exam last year.
That's the girl ...
c I told you about that boy yesterday.
That's the boy ...
d That woman is in love with me!
That's the woman ...
e That boy never tells the truth.
That's the boy ...
f I really want to meet that girl.
That's the girl ...
g I saw that man with her at the cinema.
That's the man ...
h That woman told me about them.
That's the woman ...
i That boy borrowed my cassette player.
That's the boy ...
j That girl asked me to her party.
That's the girl ...

SKILLS: LISTENING AND WRITING

Pre-writing

1 Choose one of these people and decide what you could say about him or her. Use the topics below.

appearance, physical description
family situation
home, country

work
likes and dislikes
leisure activities

Writing

2 Plan a letter to a penfriend agency. You have to describe yourself, and the kind of person you would like to have as a penfriend. In this exercise, you are the person from the picture you chose in question 1. The agency will find you a friend who fits the description you give. Use the outline below.

(your address)
(date)

Dear Penfriends Unlimited,
    I am writing to you because I would like to write to a (girl/boy) who lives in Britain.
    (describe yourself) ....
....
....
    I would like to write to someone who ....
....
....
....
    I hope to hear from you soon.
    (end the letter)

3 Collect the letters and read them all. Try to find a suitable penfriend for each person who wrote a letter.

Pre-listening

4 Explain the meanings of the words below. Check them in your dictionary if necessary.

honest
An honest person is someone who tells the truth, and also someone who obeys the law. For example, if an honest person found some money, she would take it to the police station.

patient	romantic
cheerful	lively
tolerant	helpful
a good listener	thoughtful
amusing	annoying
frank	careful

Which one best describes your friends?

Listening

5 ☎ Listen to people describing their friends. Which words in question 4 could they use to describe the friends they mention?

Check your grammar

Contractions

1 In speech, we often shorten some verb forms, but we write them in full. Study the sentences and write the forms <u>underlined</u> in full.

Speaking She said <u>she'd lost</u> her books.
Writing *She said she had lost her books.*

   a Actually I think <u>she's already left</u>.
   b He said <u>she'd gone</u> by the time he got there.
   c He says <u>he'd like</u> to see you again.
   d I think <u>you'd better</u> talk to her.
   e She says <u>she's having</u> a party next week.
   f I think <u>I'd accept</u> if he asked me.

Build your vocabulary

Colloquial expressions

1 What would you say in these situations?

   1 You want to warn someone who is in danger.
   2 You feel disappointed or upset.
   3 You want someone to go away, and you are not polite.
   4 You make a mistake when you are writing and feel angry.
   5 You are talking to someone, but you want to think for a moment.
   6 You want someone to wait for something.

2 When can you say this? Match each expression with one of the situations from question 1.

   a Hang on a moment.   **e** Excuse me!
   b Oh dear, how awful.   **f** Let me see.
   c Oh, get lost!   **g** Oh bother!
   d Look out!   **h** Pardon me!

There are two expressions which cannot be used for any of the situations. When would you say them?

Practise your pronunciation

Consonant sounds

1 How would you pronounce each group of words?

   shock/ʃɒk/   sock/sɒk/
   shore/ʃɔ:/   sore/sɔ:/
   shoe/ʃu:/   Sue/su:/
   ship/ʃɪp/   sip/sɪp/
   shy/ʃaɪ/   sigh/saɪ/

   ▭ Listen and repeat.

2 How would you pronounce these groups?

   plays/pleɪz/   place/pleɪs/
   raise/reɪz/   race/reɪs/
   prize/praɪz/   price/praɪs/
   trays/treɪz/   trace/treɪs/
   seize/si:z/   cease/si:s/

   ▭ Listen and repeat.

Unit 11 What's on?

Leisure time

1 How do you spend your free time? Complete the questionnaire.

activity	quite often	occasionally	very rarely	never
watch TV				
read a newspaper				
go to the theatre				
listen to music				
listen to the radio				
go to the cinema				
visit museums/galleries				
borrow a video film				
read a magazine				
listen to live music				
go dancing				
play a musical instrument				
go to the ballet/opera				
read a book				

Compare your results and explain your answers.

I quite often watch television if I don't have anything else to do.

2 Choose an activity for Saturday evening, and persuade someone else to join you.

▶ Passive voice
▶ Making comparisons
▶ Persuading

1 How much do you know about what happens in a television studio? Can you guess? Match the job names with the job descriptions.

a *I create the studio sets and scenery.*
b *I check the balance and level of sound from the microphones.*
c *I move parts of the scenery around the studio.*
d *I change the lights on the studio set.*
e *I give instructions to all the people working in the studio.*
f *I instruct the actors, choose the camera shots, and so on.*
g *I encourage the audience to laugh before the show begins.*
h *I take the actual shots of the actors on the studio floor.*
i *I create clothes which are worn by actors.*

costume designer
camera operator
director
lighting
  supervisor
warm-up man
scene shifter
set designer
floor manager
sound supervisor

Read through your answers again, and describe who you think is responsible for the jobs in the list.

Passive voice   6
*I think the financial decisions **are made by** the producer.*

2 Here is a list which shows some of the things which *have to be done* before the programme can be made. Put the list in order and explain what has to be done.

What is the most important job in the studio? Which is the most interesting? What skills would you need for each job?

studio audience
actors
script
make-up
studio
rehearsal
special effects
editing
financial decisions

3 What are the most popular television programmes in your country? Describe two programmes you have seen recently. Do you think they could be better?

Making comparisons with adjectives   14.1, 14.2

*Children's programmes are **not as interesting as** they could be.*
*The news could be **much more informative**.*

Superlatives   14.3

*'Dallas' is **the most entertaining** programme in my country.*
*I think 'Benny Hill' is **the funniest** foreign series.*

What do you think about television? Which of these points do you agree with?

Television

It doesn't teach people anything.
It has too many boring programmes.
It doesn't have enough for children.
It has too many soap operas.
It makes young people violent.
It has too many foreign programmes.

It is very entertaining.
It keeps us informed.
It helps us to relax.
It teaches us many things.
It shows us what other countries are like.
It makes us think.

4 Form a group of four. Choose one programme description each. Try to persuade other members of your group that your programme is most worth watching.

Starcrossed
BELINDA BAUER
JAMES SPADER

Mary is an exotic, enigmatic woman who's being pursued by mysterious twins armed with strange and powerful weapons. Emerging from a downtown bar, Joey and his friends ward off Mary's pursuers, unaware that she is an alien on the run from extra-terrestrial killers.

See film guide, beginning page 25

TELEPLAY/DIRECTOR
JEFFREY BLOOM

Go for It

The second in the series of programmes which shows just how much children with special needs can do if given the chance. Groups from all over Britain have a go at different activities from land-yachting to computer music, caving to ballet. The children talk about their adventures, their fears, aspirations and how much confidence they gain through independence. This week Sara, Marisa and friends find out how to harness the wind when they go land-yachting for the first time and Wayne, Graham and Elizabeth learn how to make puppets and put on a show. Don't forget

you can win a week away in the *Go For It* competition. For poster/ leaflet send an sae to C4 address 1, page 47.

Owl TV
MICHAELA STRACHAN

Imagine a country covered in forests and inhabited by wolves, bears, lynxes, wild boar, bison and Arctic foxes – that was northern Britain 10,000 years ago. Although these animals are extinct in the wild here now, the programme finds them all at a special park in Scotland. *The Mighty Mites* investigate a bee which makes its home in an old flower pot and *Bonapart* accompanies

Daniel to the dentist, only to find himself in the chair. Also there's a look at the Southern White rhinoceros which has been saved by captive breeding at places like San Diego Wild Animal Park.
● Keep on the wildlife track with *Owl*, the new full-colour monthly nature magazine for children. On sale now, price £1.20.
EXECUTIVE PRODUCER
(FOR OWL TV)
ANNABEL SLAIGHT
PRODUCER
(FOR THAMES TELEVISION)
DAVE ROGERS

An owl TV/Thames Television Production

Superchamps

The third exciting round to find this year's Superchamps on powerboats, motorbikes, meteors and jetskis – with a little 'expert' coaching from Gary Crowley this week as he tries out his skill on the Wonderwheel. The interviewer is Estelle Matthews, with commentary by Peter Brackley.
DIRECTOR RICK GARDENER
PRODUCERS LOUISE LEE, AVIE LITTLER
EXECUTIVE PRODUCER
JULIAN GRANT

Creative Action/MPC Television Production

Pre-reading

1 What is a musical? Do you like this kind of entertainment?

Reading

2 Scan the text and find out what the musical is about, and who performed it.

STING - AND THE CHILDREN WHO SING FOR A BETTER WORLD

1 Sting stood on the stage, bathed in spotlight, and clearly moved. The audience had risen to its feet in unison and the cries for an encore 5 echoed round the huge concert hall in Washington's Kennedy centre. [1] It was equally for the 200 children from St Augustine's School in Billington, Lancashire, who had 10 travelled to America to perform a musical, written by their music teacher, Peter Rose, after seven Sundays of six-hour rehearsals to get to the perfection of this evening.

15 Sting, a schoolteacher himself before turning professional musician, said: '[2] It was exhausting. I spent hours on the plane getting here and I've got to spend hours on the 20 plane tomorrow, but it's been worth it. I've been at school concerts before, both as a teacher and a kid, and they were always a bit out of tune. But the standards of this school 25 were staggering, and these kids knew what they were singing about. It was a magical evening.' The musical, titled *Yanomano*, which has lyrics written by another teacher, Anne 30 Conlon, [3] and recounts the terrible effects of the destruction of the world's tropical forests to make way for the rearing of cattle. Sting said pointedly: 'The Yanomano Indians 35 have lived in harmony with their environment for some 20,000 years, which is more than you can say about most of the civilised Western world.'

40 The programme is a rich mosaic depicting the terrible destruction of the world's tropical rainforests [4]. But behind that story lies the unusual commitment of a world-famous rock 45 star and 200 schoolchildren who, with 20 teachers, defied the logistical nightmare of air fares and accommodation to perform their musical before a spellbound audi-50 ence. [5] Trinity College in Washington offered its campus and, in the sweltering, humid heat, the choir and orchestra of St Augustine's sang and played their hearts out.

55 When Sting was invited to perform the narration for the show, he accepted eagerly. 'The musical was about [6] the Amazon. It began for me when I spent four hours in a tiny 60 plane flying over a vast area where serious destruction had occurred. I looked down on parched, dry desert and was told that 10 years ago, that same land had been rich forest. It 65 frightened me. [7] My contribution was a very simple one. As narrator I just had to turn up and read some lines.'

[8] Sting felt compelled to join in 70 the final chorus. Laughing, he explained: 'As a singer, I found myself tapping my foot and wanting to take part. [9] Peter Rose took me into a dressing room and taught me the 75 final verse very quickly. We just ran through it twice and although I was nervous about singing something which was only vaguely familiar [10].' And when Sting burst into 80 song, centre stage, the audience went wild.

When the school and Sting finally left the stage, applause ringing in their ears, instead of heading for the 85 privacy of his dressing room, Sting joined the children. Mutual congratulations were exchanged and backs slapped.

3 Complete the text in question 2 by putting one of the phrases or sentences into each numbered space in the text.

a Their parents raised nearly £50,000.
b But, by the end of the performance,
c I'm honoured to have been here tonight.
d a part of the world I had come to know –
e tells the story of a tribe of Indians living in the Amazon forest,
f I'm really glad I did
g But the tumultuous applause was not for Sting alone.
h It also made me very angry.
i and the implications of that for us all
j During the interval,

Word search

4 Find words in the text connected with performances which mean:

part of theatre where actors perform

people who go to see a play or film

practices for actors or singers

person who plays music

words sung to music

large group who sing together

part of a song that everyone sings

room where actors change

Comprehension check

5 Are these statements about the text **true**(t) or **false**(f)?

a Peter Rose wrote the musical on seven Sunday afternoons.
b Sting had to travel a long distance to get to the performance.
c The singing at school concerts Sting has been to was not perfect.
d Peter Rose wrote the music but another teacher wrote the words.
e The school had to pay £50,000 to use the Trinity College campus.
f Sting did not at first intend to sing in the show.

Speaking

6 Do you think that this school musical was a good idea? What did the children from St Augustine's School learn by taking part?

Pre-listening

7 Which of the following would you go and see, and why?

musical   horror film   modern ballet   school play

Listening

8 ☐ Listen to the part of a radio programme about a popular series of horror films. Which of the following points are mentioned?

a The first film was made in 1984.
b The first film was not a commercial success and lost money.
c The films were all made in the same studio in Los Angeles.
d The films are not intended to be seen by young children.
e Another attraction of the films is their lively music.
f Only people who watch a lot of home videos watch these films.
g Many children do not realise that the main character is not real.

Speaking

9 Do you enjoy films like this? Can you explain why?

Passive voice with agent ▶ 6

1 How much do you know about entertainment and the media? Choose answers for the quiz from the list below. Use a passive form in the correct tense.

*The James Bond books **were written by Ian Fleming**.*

a Who directed the film *ET*?
b Who wrote the play *Hamlet*?
c Who invented the character Sherlock Holmes?
d Who sang *Heartbreak Hotel*?
e Who played James Bond in *Goldfinger*?
f Who wrote the novel *War and Peace*?
g Who first recorded the song *Help*?
h Who invented radio?
i Who played the 'Beverley Hills Cop'?
j Who composed *The Magic Flute*?

1 The Beatles
2 Eddie Murphy
3 Leo Tolstoy
4 Steven Spielberg
5 William Shakespeare
6 Marconi
7 Sir Arthur Conan Doyle
8 W. A. Mozart
9 Elvis Presley
10 Sean Connery

Passive voice without agent ▶ 6

2 Rewrite each comment about the media beginning as shown.

Television gives us all the same opinions.
One danger of television is that we ...
One advantage of radio is that we are all given the same opinions.

a Radio entertains us wherever we are.
One advantage of radio is that we ...
b Television fills our minds with pictures of violence.
The worst thing about television is that our ...
c Newspapers give us information about other parts of the world.
One good thing about newspapers is that we ...
d Television keeps us up to date on the political situation.
Thanks to television, we ...
e Television prevents us from thinking for ourselves.
A possible danger of television is that we ...
f The news on the radio doesn't allow us to forget our problems.
If we listen to the news on the radio, we ...
g Newspapers give us different points of view about what is happening.
When we read newspapers, we ...
h Local radio makes us aware of what is happening in our area.
A great advantage of local radio is that we ...
i Going to the cinema gives us the chance to meet other people.
An advantage of going to the cinema is that we ...
j Television forces us to sit down and do nothing else.
A disadvantage of television is that we ...

Passive voice ▶ 6

3 Change each sentence so that it begins with the word underlined.

television
Television was invented by a number of different scientists and engineers.

> A number of different scientists and engineers invented television. They developed it for public use before the Second World War. Up until the outbreak of the war the BBC broadcast many programmes. They stopped the service during the war, however. By the beginning of the 1950s people had purchased many TV sets. The authorities increased the number of TV channels until there were two BBC channels and two commercial channels. Scientists also developed colour television. People pay for the BBC channels by a licence fee. Special radar vans detect people who have not paid for the licence. International companies have started satellite programmes recently.

Making comparisons ▶ 14.2

4 Compare the leisure activities using adjectives from the list.

*Television is **not as interesting as** the cinema because staying at home is rather boring. Going out is **better**.*

a novels/films of the book
b newspapers/the news on TV
c plays/films
d comic books/magazine stories
e old films/modern films
f tapes and video/books and magazines.
g pop music/classical music
h a library/a video library
i records/cassettes and CDs
j films from your country/ foreign films

entertaining
informative
relaxing

interesting
exciting
funny

good
useful
economical

Phrasal/multi-word verbs ▶ 19

5 Rewrite the text using the phrasal verbs given. Replace the words which are underlined.

bring up
come round
do without
get along with
join in

live on
keep on
send for
set off
turn up

> **BBC1 9.50**
> *Raising My Darling Daughter* stars Julie Sykes and Ken Moreland. Sue has a difficult time with her new teacher, and leaves for the cottage, where she survives on tins of beans. Ugh! And she manages without her friends for a while – until handsome Peter (Mark Dale) calls at the house. He continues calling until – surprise, surprise – they fall in love. Meanwhile Dad (Ken Moreland) asks Dr Miles (Phil Bates) to come, and he arrives suddenly at the cottage. Other local people (including some hilarious hippies) take part and the result is as usual – very funny. Don't miss it.

SKILLS: LISTENING AND WRITING

Listening

1 ☐ Listen to people being interviewed about their opinions of television programmes. In the table below, make a note of whether they **like** or **dislike** the programmes or have **no strong opinion**.

	The Summer Family	*Popsquare*	*Newsline*
Jane			
Philip			
Lisa			
Steve			

2 ☐ Listen again and <u>underline</u> any phrases listed below which you hear on the cassette. Decide whether each phrase is **positive** (+) or **negative** (−).

entertaining and lively
I can't stand Robert Weeks
the worst programme on TV
I find him really annoying
very well acted
really good entertainment

a waste of time
very informative
rather uninteresting
a really wonderful programme
badly produced
isn't as good as it used to be

Pre-writing

3 These sentences make the first paragraph of a composition. Put them in a logical order and choose a title for the composition.

As well as sport, I am interested in classical music.
Finally I also watch old films when I have time.
As I like sport a lot, I always enjoy watching sports programmes.
However, there aren't many programmes on television of this kind.
I don't watch television a lot, but I do have some favourite programmes.
Whenever there is a concert shown on television, I try to watch it.

4 Here are some possible topics for the second paragraph of this composition. Choose the one you think is best. Give your reasons.

The kinds of films I like best.
Programmes I think should be on TV.
Children's programmes.
What I do in my spare time.
What I like about sport on TV.
Programmes I don't like.
My ambitions for the future.
Other programmes I like a lot.

Writing

5 Write a composition with this title:

What kinds of television programmes do you like best? Are there any programmes which you really dislike? Give some examples.

Before you write, make a list of points you could include using some of the phrases from this page, and plan two paragraphs.

Check your grammar

Passive voice

1 Study these pairs of sentences. Can you explain what difference there is when the sentence is passive, as in sentence **2**?

a 1 A thief has stolen my bike!

    2 My bike has been stolen!

b 1 The director of the school has cancelled the holiday.

    2 The holiday has been cancelled.

c 1 The chef cooked this meat too much.

    2 This meat was cooked too much.

Build your vocabulary

Words easily confused

1 Use a dictionary to check the meaning of each pair of words. Write sentences to show that you understand the difference between the words in each pair.

a to bring up/to grow up ....

....

b to check/to control ....

....

c fees/bills ....

....

d to teach/to learn ....

....

e a play/a game ....

....

f to record/to write ....

....

Positive and negative words

2 a Which of these words could be used to describe a book, play, film or piece of music?

slow	violent
well-acted	disturbing
informative	loud
confusing	realistic

b Decide whether the words in **a** have **positive** (+) or **negative** (−) meanings. Can any be used in both senses?

Practise your pronunciation

Intonation and meaning

1 🔊 Listen to the intonation of the questions given. Each question will be spoken twice, with different answers.

a What did you think of the film?

b Do you buy many books?

c Who wrote the play?

d Do you like modern jazz?

e What kind of music do you like best?

🔊 Listen again, and imitate the questions and answers.

STARTING POINTS

Planning your home

1 Which room do you like best? Can you explain why?

2 You are a famous film star or singer. You want to live in an unusual house in Hollywood with your family. Make a plan to show to your architect. Use the sketch plan to decide how you want your house to be organised.

I want all the bedrooms to be near the swimming pool.

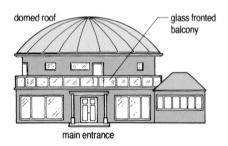

Two floors

domed roof — glass fronted balcony

main entrance

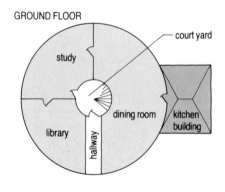

GROUND FLOOR

court yard

study

dining room

kitchen building

library

hallway

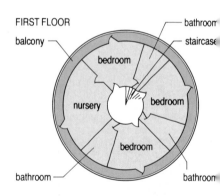

FIRST FLOOR

balcony — bathroom — staircase

bedroom

nursery — bedroom

bedroom

bathroom — bathroom

Give an explanation for each part of your plan.

3 Decide where exactly in the house these things should be. Explain your reasons.

LANGUAGE ACTIVITIES

▶ Stating preferences
▶ Comparing past and present
▶ Suggesting changes

1 What sort of town or village do you live in? What good points and bad points does it have?
Is it better to live in a town or in a village? Describe the advantages and disadvantages.

2 Look at the pictures and talk about which place you prefer. Explain your reasons.

Living in a town	**Living in a village**
advantages	advantages
disadvantages	disadvantages

Stating preferences 8.12

I'd rather live in the centre of a town **than** in a village. There is more social life.
I'd prefer to live in a village because it's quieter.
It would be better to live in the country if you had children. There is more room for them to play.

---

3 These pictures show a town as it used to be, and as it is now. Study the pictures and find the following places:

cottage   shop   railway   housing estate
inn   field   farm   motorway

1950

NOW

Describe the differences between the two pictures.

Would you rather live in the old town shown in the illustration, or the town as it is today? Give your reasons.

4 Read this extract from a letter to a newspaper and make a list of five similar problems in your town.

> Sir,
> I am writing to complain yet again about the way the town council has done absolutely nothing to solve the many problems facing this town. There is always a traffic jam in the High Street and it's impossible to find anywhere to park. And our children have to play in the streets because there is nowhere else for them to go.

Read the second extract from the letter and suggest some solutions to the problems in your list.

> Is this what we pay our taxes for? There are so many things which could be done. For a start, most traffic should be banned from the city centre. And so many things could be done for our young people. I suggest that a sports centre could be built on the empty site in Haverstock Road, so that people would have somewhere to go to keep fit.

> **Describing change**
>
> **Passive voice   6**
>
> ***There used to be*** lots of trees, but they ***have been cut down.***
> ***There didn't use to be*** a cinema.
> A new block of flats ***has been built*** on the corner.

SKILLS: READING AND LISTENING

Pre-listening

1 Would you like to live in an unusual house? What might be good, or bad, about living in one of these places?

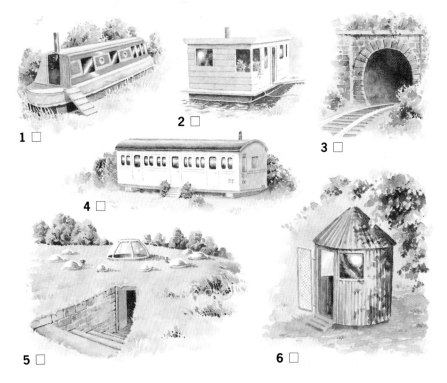

Listening

2 📼 Listen to people talking about their unusual homes. Tick (✓) the pictures in question 1 which show the places they are talking about.

3 📼 Listen again and decide whether the statements below are **true** (t) or **false** (f).

- **a** 1 The boat does not actually float on the water.
  - 2 The man speaking turned the boat into a house.
- **b** 1 The house was built because it was cheaper this way.
  - 2 They also have a garden inside the house.
- **c** 1 Some parts of the house are still empty.
  - 2 Guests sometimes worry that trains will come through the house.
- **d** 1 The woman who lives in the house has recently sold it.
  - 2 She now lives in an old bathroom with her cat.

Speaking

4 You are trying to sell one of the houses you heard described in question 3. Describe its good points. Try to make it sound interesting.

Pre-reading

5 Read the estate agent's description of a house. For each phrase <u>underlined</u>, choose a phrase below which explains what the house is really like.

> A house of <u>character</u> in the countryside ten miles from Bath. A fine example of <u>innovative restoration</u> placed among trees and with views of the River Avon. Reception, dining-room, 4 bedrooms, kitchen, 2 bathrooms. All ground floor rooms have <u>double aspect</u>, and the house is fully carpeted. <u>A modern construction</u>, which has been thoroughly redecorated and <u>sympathetically modernised</u> to create a delightful family home. Solid fuel central heating. [Extras include swimming pool in garden, and brick-built dog kennel.] A bargain at £200,000. View by appointment only. **Graham and Sons, Estate Agents.**

- **a** a house built in the last fifty years
- **b** the windows look in two different directions
- **c** a very unusual house
- **d** it has been made more up-to-date but not spoiled
- **e** it has been changed in an unusual way

Reading

6 Read the article about the bus in the picture and complete the plan below. What would it be like to live in this bus?

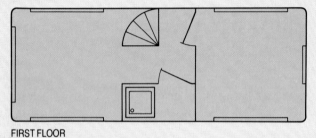

£40,000 TO TAKE A BUS HOME

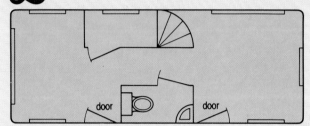

GROUND FLOOR

FIRST FLOOR

1 With this one-bedroom flat you have to read between the lines of the estate agent's particulars even more carefully than usual, Stephen Ward writes. It is 'a modern construction home of character being a truly magnificent example of innovative restoration and sympathetic modernisation'. Offers are invited
5 around £40,000.
  That sounds a bargain as you read on. The entrance vestibule with side hand-rails and double electric doors leads to a lobby with stairs to the first floor. On the ground floor the fully-fitted kitchen has a view on three sides, a 'triple aspect' as the estate agents say. A study has space for a chair, they say
10 hopefully. A separate WC has its own sink. The dining room has a 'double aspect' and space to seat seven. Up the spiral staircase to the first floor, there is a shower room and another triple aspect room called, intriguingly, a TV/ Observation lounge, with a wine cabinet and bookshelves. Finally we come to the bedroom. 'Fully carpeted,' the agents gush. 'Gas-fired central-heating. Air-
15 conditioning'. Then a clue: 'original bell'. For sale is a 1976 double-decker bus, converted by an enthusiast who used it for holidays in Britain. The present owners bought it in February, planning to tour Europe this summer. When they were unable to, they decided to sell it. 'It was a moot point whether to sell it through a mobile home dealer or an estate agent,' Lesley Aspinall, of
20 Hitchcocks, the south London estate agents selling the bus, said. The bus would be better for someone short as the ceilings upstairs are not more than 1.75m high. If you try to live in it in the Battersea street where it is parked, or in any other public place, the police will move you on. And an owner would need a heavy goods licence to be allowed to drive it.
25 Miss Aspinall is still waiting for the first offer.

Comprehension check

7 Underline information in the text which shows why the people described below would probably not find this home suitable.

  a Someone who is over two metres tall.
  b Two students who wanted a quiet place to study.
  c Someone who has a driving licence for a car.
  d Someone who doesn't have a house in the city and wants to live in the centre.
  e A family with three young children.

Speaking

8 What kind of person might want to live in a bus? Can we learn anything about someone's character from their house?

GRAMMAR PRACTICE

Passive voice: tense contrasts ▶ 6

1 You are moving house today. Complete each comment using a passive form of the verb in brackets.

The kitchen things (put) in boxes yesterday?
[past simple/present perfect]
*Were the kitchen things **put** in boxes yesterday?*   past simple

a The car (service) today! How are we going to get there? In the van?
[present simple/present continuous]

b The removal men (tell) to be here at 8.00am – late! Here at 9.00!
[present simple/present perfect simple/past simple]

c I'm sure those vases (break). Tell the men to be careful.
[present simple/future/present perfect]

d My books (pack) yet? I want them to go in these boxes.
[past simple/ present perfect/future]

e The removal company say that things always (pack) carefully.
[present simple/past simple/present perfect]

f The electricity not (cut off) yet, so we can make some tea.
[present continuous/present perfect/past simple]

g Our letters (send on) to the new address from now on, according to the postman.
[future/present perfect/past simple]

h If anything (leave behind), we can always go and pick it up later.
[present simple/past simple/present perfect]

i The gas (cut off) yesterday morning, so that's not a worry.
[present continuous/present perfect/past simple]

j The men (pay) by the hour, so let's get the job done quickly!
[present simple/past simple/present perfect]

2 Read the comments below, and decide what *has/has not been done*. Write a sentence using the verb given in brackets.

There is water coming through the roof!   (repair)
The roof hasn't been repaired.

a The walls in the living room are really dirty! (wash)

b The small bedroom still has that horrible green door.   (paint)

c We asked for a radiator in the hall, but there isn't one.   (install)

d The back door is still broken and doesn't close properly.   (repair)

e The kitchen was supposed to be painted blue, not brown.   (paint)

f Where's the garden wall? We want to keep that! (knock down)

g But we wanted you to get rid of the garden shed. (remove)

h In the plans, there is a third window in the kitchen. (put in)

i What happened to the lovely apple tree outside the back door?   (cut down)

j There's builder's rubbish everywhere!   (take away)

Prepositions of place and position ▶ 18

3 Study the illustration of the room and complete the sentences below.

*The sink is **next to** the fridge.*

a There's some cat food _____ a tin _____ the fridge.
b The sugar is _____ the jar _____ the tea and the coffee.
c The stool is _____ the table _____ the window.
d The knives and forks are _____ the second drawer.
e There are some biscuits _____ the tin _____ the top shelf.
f _____ the cupboard _____ the fridge there's a teapot.
g The jam is _____ the honey _____ the bottom shelf.
h There's a bucket _____ the cupboard _____ the sink.

Street puzzle

4 Study the street map, and the information below. Fill in the names of the people.

_____	Sally	_____	_____	_____	_____
37	39	41	43	45	47

_____	_____	you	_____	_____	_____
36	38	40	42	44	46

a Alice lives next door to you.
b Bill lives opposite Sally.
c Janet lives next door to Joe.
d Harry lives opposite Alice.
e Joe lives next door to Harry.
f Jean lives next door to Sally.
g Liz lives opposite Jean.
h Malcolm lives opposite Janet.
i Pete lives between Harry and Sally.
j Which house is empty?

5 Where exactly would you put these household objects? Describe their position, and which room they would be in.

curtains
*You hang them **in front of** the windows, **in** any room.*

cooker	dishwasher
carpet	towel
shelves	pillow
settee	pillow
bookcase	cushion
wardrobe	lamp

SKILLS: LISTENING AND WRITING

Listening

1 📼 Listen to two descriptions of places to live. As you listen, tick (✓) the pictures which show these places. Complete the information in the table.

1 ☐ 2 ☐ 3 ☐ 4 ☐

	first house	second house
Location:	....	....
Type:	....	....
No. of rooms:	....	*6 bedrooms*
	....	....
Facilities:	....	....
	....	....
Transport:	*near the Underground*	....
Facilities nearby:	....	....

2 📼 Listen again and make notes about the advantages and disadvantages of each house.

Role play

3

Student A	Student B
Persuade your partner that the first house is the best. Point out its advantages and compare it with the second house. Use the notes you made in question 2.	Persuade your partner that the second house is the best. Point out its advantages and compare it with the first house. Use the notes you made in question 2.

Writing

4 Write about **one** of the houses, using ideas you discussed in question 2. Use this paragraph outline.

This house has many advantages. First of all ....
....
....
As well as this, ...
....
....
Another advantage is ....
....
....

On the other hand, there are some disadvantages. The main one is that ....
....
....
Besides this, ...
....
....
Another problem is that ....
....
....

Although there are some disadvantages, I would rather live in this house, because ......
....
....

5 Write a description of the house you live in, or would like to live in. Before you write, talk about your description with other students.

STUDY FOCUS

Check your grammar

1 Study the sentences below, and decide which ones refer to **now** (offers and preferences) and which ones refer to **always** (opinions).

    a I'd like some tea, please.
    b Do you like coffee?
    c Would you like another cake?
    d I'd prefer a biscuit, please.
    e I prefer coffee.
    f Which would you like, coffee or tea?
    g I think I'd rather have a glass of water.
    h Which do you prefer, coffee or tea?

Build your vocabulary

Word formation

1 Use the dictionary to complete these lists.

adjective	verb	noun
wide	_____	_____
long	_____	_____
deep	_____	_____
high	_____	_____

Words easily confused

2 Explain the difference between these pairs of words. Write a sentence for each one to make the meaning clear.

    a cooker/cook
    b cushion/pillow
    c motorway/road
    d a room/some room
    e sink/washbasin
    f van/lorry

Practise your pronunciation

Unstressed syllables

1 How would you pronounce these words? Pay attention to the parts **in bold**.

    a condi**tion**
       posi**tion**
       ambi**tion**
       accommoda**tion**
       popula**tion**
       decora**tion**
       educa**tion**
       pollu**tion**

    b capi**tal**
       can**dle**
       remo**val**
       chan**nel**
       economi**cal**
       finan**cial**
       han**dle**
       hos**tel**

    Listen and repeat.

Grammar Reference

These pages give more detailed grammatical explanations, and include reference material, for points you need to know at this level.

1 Present simple and present continuous

1.1 Present simple

Form I/you/we/they **live**.
He/she/it **lives**.
Do you live here? **Does** he live here?
I **don't** live here. She **doesn't** live here.

Use 1 For a state, unlimited by time.

> She **lives** in Chelsea.
> He **knows** a lot about cars.

2 For a routine, or habit.

> They **get up** every morning at eight.
> He always **comes** late.

3 For things that are always true.

> Water **freezes** at zero degrees Centigrade.

1.2 Frequency adverbs

These tell us how often an event happens.

always usually often sometimes rarely never

They are placed between subject and verb.

*We **always** have steak for dinner on Friday.*

They follow auxiliary verbs, and the verb *to be*.

*He is **usually** here at this time.*
*I have **never** seen a poisonous snake.*

Usually, often and *sometimes* are also common at the beginning and end of clauses.

Sometimes I wonder why I talk to you at all!

1.3 Present continuous

Form You/we/they **are waiting**.
He/she/it **is waiting**.
I **am waiting**.
Are they waiting? **Is** she waiting?
She **isn't** waiting. They **aren't** waiting.

Use 1 For an event happening at the moment of speaking.

> She**'s eating** her breakfast.

2 For a state made to seem more temporary.

> He**'s living** with relatives at the moment.

3 Time expressions commonly used with the present continuous are *at the moment* and *now*.

1.4 Future reference

Present tenses can also refer to future time (See 4.4)

1.5 Verbs not normally used in continuous

Some verbs cannot normally be used in the continuous form. Verbs mainly used only in the simple form are:

1 *Know, understand, believe, think* and verbs with similar meanings.
2 *Own, cost, belong to, contain, depend* and similar verbs.
3 Verbs of sensation such as *see, hear* and *smell,* are often used with *can* or *could*.

2 Past simple, past continuous, *used to*

2.1 Past simple

Form **Regular**
I/you/he/she/it/we/they **decided**.
Did he decide? They **didn't** decide.
Irregular
I/you/he/she/it/we/they **left**.
Did she leave? We **didn't** leave.

Use

1 For a finished event in the past.

   *I **bought** a new bike last week.*

2 For narratives and stories.

   *We **left** New York and **flew** to Chicago.*

3 For past habits.

   *I usually **went** to the cinema every Saturday.*

2.2 Past continuous

Form   I/he/she/it **was eating**.
We/you/they **were eating**.
Was he eating?   **Were** they eating?
I **wasn't** eating.   We **weren't** eating.

Use

1 For a long, unfinished action in contrast with a sudden, complete one. This is sometimes an interruption.

   *While I **was cooking** the dinner, the phone rang.*

2 For background action in a narrative, in contrast with the main narrative events.

   *A lot of people **were standing** outside, shouting. Some of them **were waving** banners. I parked the car, and watched.*

Note: it is NOT used to describe a habit in the past.

2.3 *Used to*

Form   I/you/he/she/it/we/they **used to play** tennis.
Did you **use to** play?
I **didn't use to** play.

Use

1 *Used to* refers to past time and has NO PRESENT FORM.
2 It describes a habitual action which has now finished, often in contrast with the present.

   *I **used to play** tennis, but I don't have the time now.*
   *I **didn't use to like** jazz, but now I do.*

Note: the pronunciation of *used to* is / juːs tə/.

3 Present perfect simple and continuous

3.1 Present perfect simple

Form   I/you/we/they **have decided**.
He/she/it **has decided**.
Have you decided?   I **haven't** decided.
Has she decided?   She **hasn't** decided.

Use

1 For states starting in the past and lasting until the present.

   *How long **have you known** him?*
   *I've **known** him for twenty years.*
   *I've **known** him since 1987.*

   Note: *for* + period of time.
   since + beginning of period.

2 For an event in the past, for which no definite time is given.

   *I've **visited** Rome twice.*

3 For an indefinite event which we think of as being very recent.

   *The shop on the corner **has closed**.*

4 Where we feel that the result of an event is still present.

   *The electricity **has gone off**.*
   The lights are still out.

3.2 Present perfect continous

Form   I/you/we/they **have been working**.
He/she/it **has been working**.
Have you been working?
Has she been working?
He **hasn't** been working.
They **haven't** been working.

Use

1 To suggest that an action starting in the past has only just finished, or may continue.

   *I've **been cleaning** the house all day.*
   I'm still holding the broom.

2 To show the length of the action starting in the past.

   *I've **been waiting** for you for hours.*

3 To show incompleteness. Compare:

I've been reading that book you lent
me.   (not finished)
I've read that book you lent
me.   (finished)

4 To show a repeated activity.

I've been going to the theatre a lot lately.

4 Future time

4.1 *Will*

Form   I/you/he/she/it/we/they **will stay**.
Will she stay?
He **will not** stay.
Short forms
'll = will   **won't** = will not
Note: *shall* can be used with *I* and *we* but
is not common for referring to
future time. It is used to make
offers and suggestions.

Use   1 To make a prediction.

*I think it **will rain** tomorrow.*
*Soon there **won't be** any oil left.*

2 See the list of Language Functions for
other common uses of *will* and *shall*:
8.4, 8.9, 8.13.

4.2 *Going to*

Use   1 To show a plan or intention.

*They're **going to buy** a house in Leeds.*

2 To make a prediction based on the
beginning or the cause of the event.

*Look at that crazy driver! He **is going to
crash!***
He can't stop in time.

4.3 Future continuous

Form   I/you/he/she/it/we/they **will be
leaving**.
I/we **shall be leaving**   (See 4.1)
I **won't** be leaving.
Will she be leaving?

Use   For a temporary action (as in the present
continuous) but related to a point in the
future.

*At the moment I **am working** in my
office.   (present)*
*This time next week I'**ll be lying** on the
beach.   (future)*

4.4 Future use of present continuous

Present continuous can be used to refer to the
future for a fixed arrangement, one written in a
diary, for example.
This is very common when describing social
arrangements, and is often used with verbs of
motion such as *come* and *go*. A time expression
is usually used to make the meaning clear.

*What **are you doing** on Saturday?*
*I'**m going** to France this summer.*

5 Conditionals 1 and 2, if ... sentences, and future time clauses

5.1 Conditional 1: real situations (present)

Form   In the 'if' clause, the verb has a present
tense form but does not refer to present
time. The second clause uses *will*.

*If I **miss** the train, I'**ll be** late.*

Use   This kind of sentence describes the
consequences or results of a possible
action in a situation which is real.

*If he **steps** on that branch, it **will break**.*

5.2 Conditional 2: hypothetical or imaginary situations (present/future)

Form   In the 'if' clause, the verb has a past tense
form, but refers to hypothetical or 'unreal'
time. The second clause uses the form
would + the infinitive without *to*, which is
the same form for all persons.

*If I **knew** the answer, I **would** (I'd) **tell**
you.*

111

Use 1 This kind of sentence describes the consequences or results of an imaginary action.

*If I **had** a car, I **would drive** you home.*
I have not got a car, so I cannot drive you home.

*If she **lived** here, she **could help** us.*
She does not live here, so she cannot help us.

2 The difference between Conditional 1 and 2 can depend on the attitude of the speaker.

*If that branch **breaks**, you **will fall**.*
I think it really might break!

*If that branch **broke**, you **would fall**.*
I am describing a possible situation.

3 For the verb *to be*, the form *were* (instead of *was*) can be used for all persons. This is generally considered more formal.

*If you **were** better qualified, we **would give** you the job.*

5.3 *If ...* sentences

Use 1 For things which always happen.

*If you **press** this button, an alarm **rings**.*

2 For instructions.

*If you **see** Janet, **give** her this money.*

5.4 Future time clauses

1 After some time expressions; *when, as soon as, until, before, after,* with a verb referring to the future, a present tense form is used.

*I'll see you **when** you **come back**.*
*He'll phone you **as soon as** he **arrives**.*

2 A present perfect form is also possible. This emphasises the completion of the action.

*I'll wait here **until** you **have finished**.*

6 Passive voice

Form The passive is formed with the verb *to be* and the past participle.
present simple
Many cars **are stolen** every year.
present continuous
She **is being taught** by her mother.
past simple
All the cakes **were eaten**.
past continuous
The tree **was being shaken** by the wind.
present perfect
He **has been arrested**.
infinitive   to be finished   (present)
The film **could be finished**.
They **have to be finished** at eight.

Use The passive puts more emphasis on the action rather than the person performing the action, the agent.

***They found** the jewels.*   (active)
*The jewels **were found**.*   (passive)

1 We do not usually include the agent unless this is important. Often it is obvious who performed the action, so there is no need to include it. If the agent is an unknown person, we usually leave it out.

*My bike **has been stolen**.*   (unknown agent)
*The thief **has been arrested**.*   (obviously by the police)
*The thief **was arrested by his uncle**.*   (important information)

2 Some verbs can have an object (transitive), others cannot have an object (intransitive). Intransitive verbs cannot be made passive.

He arrived at the hotel.   (intransitive)

Arrive cannot have a direct object, so it cannot be made passive.
We CANNOT say:
~~The hotel was arrived at by him.~~

7 Reported speech

7.1 Reported statements

Form   Reported speech is introduced by a verb of speaking. This is usually a past tense verb.

present – past
'I always **eat** fish.' – He said (that) he always **ate** fish.
future – *would*
'I'**ll try** it.' – She said she **would try** it.
past – past perfect
'I **ate** it.' – She said she **had eaten** it.
present perfect – past perfect
'I'**ve lost** it.' – He said he **had lost** it.
must
'I **must leave**.' – She said she **had to leave**./She said she **must leave**.
can
'I **can drive**.' – He said he **could drive**.
may
'I **may leave**.' – He said that he **might leave**.

Note: *would, could, might, ought* and *should* do not change.
The verbs in conditional 2 sentences do not change.

1 As the speaker's point of view has changed, it is usually necessary to change first and second person pronouns (*I, you*) to third person pronouns (*he, she, they*).

   'I'*ll always love* **you**,' *he said.*
   He said **he** *would always love* **her**.

2 References to place and time which involve 'here and now' are changed.

   '*I'll be* **here tomorrow**,' *she said.*
   She said she would be **there the next day**.

3 Other common changes are:
   yesterday   the day before, the previous day
   next week – the following week
   a week ago – a week before
   now   – then, at that moment

   this   – that
   these – those
   here – there
   today – that day

4 It is also possible to report with a verb in the present tense, when reporting immediately, or when referring to something which the speaker thinks is 'always true'.

   Peggy **says** *that* **she's coming round tonight**.
   The speaker has just finished talking to Peggy.

   Steve **says** *he* **likes** *you*.
   The speaker is referring to what is 'always true'.

7.2 Reported questions

1 *Yes/no* questions.

   '*Do you know the answer?*'
   She asked me **if I knew** *the answer*.

2 *Wh-* questions.

   '*What is the answer?*'
   She asked me **what the answer was.**

   Note: in both cases these are no longer direct questions, so there is no question mark, and question forms of verbs are not used.

3 Indirect questions.
   These are questions introduced by other phrases but the questions have not been spoken. They follow the same rules for reported questions.

7.3 Reporting verbs and paraphrasing

1 Many reporting verbs paraphrase the words spoken, and the actual words do not appear in reported speech.

   '*I I were you, I'* **d see** *a doctor.*'
   She advised me **to see** *a doctor.*
   '*Do you think you* **could open** *the door?*'
   He asked me **to open** *the door.*

113

2 This is a list of some common reporting verbs.

'I like you.'
She **said** (that) she liked me.
'I like you.'
She **told me** (that) she liked me.
'Go away!'
She **told me** to go away.   (an order)
'Please open the door.'
She **asked** me to open the door.
She **asked me** if I would open the door.   (a request)
'Take a seat.'
He **offered** me a seat.
'I'll help you.'
He **offered** to help me.
'I won't help you.'
He **refused** to help me.
'OK, I'll help you.'
She **agreed** to help me.
'I'll help you.'
She **promised** to help me.
'I'll buy it.'
He **decided** to buy it.
'Let's take a bus.'
I **suggested** taking a bus.
I **suggested** (that) we took a bus.
'I'm sorry I'm late.'
He **apologised** for being late.
'I think you should wait.'
I **advised** him to wait.

8 Language functions

In this list are some ways of using language for particular purposes. Not all possibilities are included. The language we use will also depend on the person we are talking to, the situation etc.

8.1 Describing ability

She can run really fast.
Do you know how to use a computer?

Know how to is often used to describe an ability which has been learned.

I'm good at swimming.

8.2 Giving advice

If I were you, I'd wait till tomorrow.
I think you should see a doctor.
You really ought to give up smoking.
Why don't you go by train?
It might be better if you rang first.

8.3 Apologising

I'm awfully sorry.
I'm sorry I'm late.
I'm sorry about forgetting/I'm sorry I forgot your birthday.

8.4 Making a decision

Thanks for the money. I'm going to buy a new coat.
This is a decision about the future, or a plan.

I'll take this one, please.
This is a decision made about the present moment, when you decide to buy something in a shop, for instance.

8.5 Giving directions

Go along this street and turn left at the church.
You go down this road, and it's a large building on the corner.

Note: *will* is not used in giving directions.

8.6 Making an introduction

John, can I introduce you to Pam?
John, this is Pam.

8.7 Inviting

Would you like to come to my party?

8.8 Describing likes and dislikes

These verbs are all followed by *-ing*, or by a noun:

enjoy   like   love   (not) mind   hate   can't stand

I really love swimming.

I can't stand cold tea.

I don't mind refers to a habitual action.

I don't mind getting up early.

Compare the use of *would you mind?* (See Requests, 8.14)

8.9 Making an offer

Shall I carry it for you?
I'll do the washing up, (shall I?)
Can I do the washing up for you?

8.10 Giving orders and instructions

Add an egg and beat thoroughly.
Leave the parcel on the table.

8.11 Asking for permission

Can I use the phone?

The following forms are considered more polite, and can be used with people you do not know well, or for more important topics.

May I go now?
Is it all right if I use your phone?
Do you think I could borrow your car?

8.12 Stating preferences

I'd rather live in the centre than in a suburb.
I'd prefer to live in the centre.
I like coffee more than tea. (in general)
I'd like coffee, please. (now)

8.13 Making a promise and making an arrangement.

I'll pay you back the money on Tuesday. (promise)
I'll see you tomorrow. (arrangement)

8.14 Making a request

Do you think you could open the window?
Would you mind closing the door?

8.15 Making a suggestion

Why don't we go to the cinema?
How about going to the cinema?
What about having a cup of tea?

9 Obligation

9.1 *Must* and *have to*

1 The difference between *must* and *have to* is very small in some cases, but one difference is that *must* expresses an obligation which comes from the speaker (a personal opinion), while *have to* expresses an obligation from someone else (a rule, for example).

   *I **must give up** drinking coffee.*
   This is my opinion.
   *I **have to give up** drinking coffee.*
   My doctor told me to.

2 There are problems of meaning, and form with *must* and *have to*, especially in negative and past tense forms.

   Negative
   *You **mustn't take** notes.*
   It is forbidden.
   *You **don't have to take** notes.*
   It is not necessary.

   Past forms
   There is no past tense of *must*. *Have to* forms are used.

   *I **had to leave** my car in the car park.*

3 For other meanings of *must*, see 10.2.

9.2 *Should*

Should is a weaker obligation.

*You **should go** now.*
It would be a good idea.

It is often used as a personal opinion about courses of action.

*I think you **should see** a doctor.*
*They **should repair** the roads.*

9.3 *Ought to*

Ought to generally has the same meaning as *should* and is used in the same way.

*We **ought to leave** before eight.*

9.4 *Had better*

Had better refers to the present, NOT the past. It generally has the same meaning as *ought to*. It is followed by the infinitive without *to*. The *had* part does not change. *Not* follows *better*.

*I'd **better do** the shopping today.*
I think I should do it today.

*You'd **better not wake up** the dog.*

10 Possibility and certainty

10.1 Possibility: *might, could*

Might and *could* express possibility.

*It **might rain** tomorrow. This **could be** a problem.*

Might can be used with *not*.

*It **might not rain**.*

10.2 Certainty: *must, can't*

Must expresses certainty. The opposite is *can't*.

*You **must know** John Knowles.*
I'm certain you do.
*You **can't know** John Knowles!*
I'm certain you don't.

11 Relative clauses

11.1 Subject and object clauses

1 If the relative pronoun (*who, that, which*) is the object of the clause, it can be left out.

*That's **the girl (who) I met** yesterday.*

2 If the relative pronoun is the subject of the clause, it cannot be left out.

*That's **the girl who used to work** here.*

3 Normally *who* refers to people, and *which* to things. In everyday speech, both are often replaced with *that*.

12 Purpose clauses

12.1 Infinitive of purpose

1 If the action, and the explanation of its purpose, have the same subject, the infinitive can be used to express purpose.

*We went to France on holiday **to study French**.*

If the person who is the subject of the purpose is mentioned in the action, then infinitive of purpose can be used.

*I've left **you** some money **to buy** a pizza.*

12.2 *So that ... can/could*

1 If the subjects are different, a *so that* clause is used.

We *went to France on holiday* **so that the children could** *study French.*

2 *So that ... can/could* can be used if the subjects are the same.

I went to France **so (that) I could study** *French.*

Note: It is possible to leave out *that.*

13 Result clauses

13.1 *So* and *such ... that*

1 *So* is used with an adjective without a noun.

The weather was **so hot** *that we went for a swim.*

2 *Such* is used with an adjective and noun. If the noun has an article, it is included.

It was **such a warm day** *that we went for a swim.*

13.2 *Too* and *not ... enough*

1 *Too* and *not* (adjective) *enough* suggest that the speaker has a result in mind.

It's **too** *hot.*
... so I can't do what I want to do.
You **aren't** *old* **enough**.
... so you can't see this film.

Note position of the adjective *old.*

2 *Too* and *not ... enough* are often followed by the infinitive with *to.*

You are **too young** *to go camping on your own.*

3 *Too* and *not ... enough* can also be followed by *for.*

This pullover is **too big for** *me.*

4 *Too* and *very* are easily confused. *Too* suggests that something cannot be done.

It's **too cold** *today to go swimming.*
It's **very cold** *today, colder than usual.*

14 Comparatives and superlatives

14.1 Forming adjectives with *-er* and *more*

1 Adjectives of one syllable usually add *-er* to form the comparative. If they end in a single consonant, with a single vowel before it, they double the final consonant.
Words ending in *-e* add *-r* only.
*long – long**er*** *fit – fi**tter***
*strange – strang**er***

2 Two syllable adjectives usually use *more*, unless they end in *-er*, *-y*, *-ow* or *-le*. Words ending in a consonant and *-y* change *-y* to *-i*.
*happy – happ**ier*** *gentle – gentl**er***
exact – **more** *exact*

3 Adjectives of three syllables or more use *more*.

14.2 Making comparisons

This chair is **more comfortable than** *that one.*
She is not **as happy as** *she used to be.*
That film was **less interesting than** *the Italian one.*

14.3 Superlatives

1 These are formed with adjective + *-est*, or *most* + adjective. The formation rules follow those given for comparative adjectives in 14.1.

2 Superlatives compare one thing in a group with all the other things in the same group.

This is **the most expensive** *restaurant* **in the town**.

This compares one restaurant with all the other restaurants.

14.4 Irregular adjectives

Adjective	Comparative	Superlative
good	*better*	*(the) best*
bad	*worse*	*(the) worst*
far	*farther*	*(the) farthest*

This is my **elder** *sister.*
My sister is **older than me**.

15 Countables and uncountables

'Countable' describes words which can have plurals. These words are sometimes also called 'units'.
'Uncountable' describes words which cannot normally have plurals. They are sometimes called 'mass' words.

15.1 Countables: *many, a few, too much/many, not enough*

Here are some examples of uncountables.

Substances:	*water milk wood stone*
Activities:	*work homework dancing*
Ideas:	*love anger happiness*
Others:	*advice money hair furniture information*

Uncountables are used with *some* if the meaning is quantity.

*Give me **some** milk, please.*
If the meaning is in general; no article is used.
I like milk.

1 *Much* and *many* are normally used with *not*, and *a lot of/lots of* is normally used for affirmative ideas. Compare these examples.

   *There were **lots of people** there.*   (everyday English)
   *There were **many people** there.*   (more formal)

2 These examples include countables.

   *We haven't got **many** clean plates.*
   *There aren't **enough** chairs.*
   *There are **only a few** biscuits left.*
   *I ate **too many** cakes.*

3 *Few* without the article has a negative idea. Compare:

   *I have **a few** friends.*
   This is a positive idea, I'm glad.
   *I have **few** friends.*
   This is a negative idea, I'm unhappy.

15.2 Uncountables: *much, little, too much/little, not enough*

1 These examples include uncountables.

   *There isn't **much** milk in the fridge.*
   *There isn't **enough** meat.*
   *There is **only a little** whisky left.*
   *There's **too much** talking.*

2 *Little* without the article has a negative idea.

   *We have **a little** time.*   some, perhaps enough
   *We have **little** time.*   not enough

16 Articles

16.1 Zero article

1 Uncountables cannot have an indefinite article (*a/an*).

   I bought some furniture.
   Give me some information.

2 Things described in general (collections, ideas) do not have a definite article (*the*).

   I like apples.
   Silence is wonderful.
   Swimming is easy.

16.2 Indefinite article

This is necessary when referring to jobs.

*She is **a** dress designer.*
*He works as **an** engineer.*

16.3 Definite article

1 This is necessary when referring to the playing of musical instruments.

   *He plays **the** piano.*
   *She is learning to play **the** violin.*

2 There is a difference between referring to a building or place only, and to its use. These places include *hospital, school, prison, church, university,* and *bed*.

> *He's at school.*
> He's having a lesson.
> *Meet me at **the** school.*
> Meet me at the building.

3 In geography, there is no article before names of towns, streets, lakes, continents and countries.

> *He lives in Italy, near Lake Como.*

There are some exceptions. Plural countries, and countries whose names contain a noun, have a definite article.

> *She lives in **the** Netherlands.*
> *He visited **the** Soviet Union last year.*

17 Time expressions

This list includes common prepositions and adverbs.

17.1 *Ago*

This refers to a point of time in the past.

> *United won the Cup six years **ago**.*

Now it is 1993, they won it in 1987.

17.2 *All*

> ***all** day/night/morning/afternoon*
> *I was awake **all** night.*

17.3 *At*

Hours of the day and night.

at six o'clock/midday/midnight/lunchtime

Periods of time.

at night

(but: *in the daytime/**during** the day, in the morning/afternoon*)

Holiday periods.

at Christmas/Easter

Beginnings and endings.

at first/last
at the beginning/end of the film

17.4 *Before*

> *We went for a drink **before** the film.*

17.5 *By*

> *I'll be here **by** three o'clock.*
> I don't know exactly when, but not after three o'clock.

17.6 *During*

> *There was a storm **during** the night.*
> This is an event which happened as part of another event.

17.7 *For*

> This refers to a period of time.
> *She went to Holland **for** three weeks.*

> This is how long she stayed there.
> Compare *ago*, and *since*.

> *She went to Holland three weeks **ago**.*
> This is when she went there.

> *She has been in Holland **since** January 5th*
> This is when she started to stay there.

17.8 *From*

> *I waited **from** two o'clock until/to half past three.*

17.9 *In*

> Periods of time, including years, seasons, months and parts of the day.

> ***in** the morning/afternoon/evening*
> ***in** January/summer/1990*

Future time.

> *I'll see you **in** two hours' time.*

119

17.10 *Just*

*He has **just** left, I'm afraid.*
This happened a few moments ago.

17.11 *Lately*

This describes a period of time up until now.

*I haven't been feeling well **lately**.*

17.12 *On*

Days and dates.

***On** Monday/Christmas Day/July 2nd*

17.13 *Recently*

*They moved house **recently**.* (not a long time ago)

17.14 *Since*

*I've been here **since** last Friday.*

See also the use of *for* and *ago*.

17.15 *Until, till*

*I'm staying here **until** Thursday.*
*I'll be here **till** eight o'clock.*

18 Prepositions of place and movement

18.1 *Above* and *over*

Both *over* and *above* can mean 'higher than'.
Over can mean 'covering'.

*The cliff rose hundreds of metres **above** us.*
*A huge bird was flying **over** our heads.*

18.2 *Among*

This is used when there are more than two things involved.

*The house was hidden **among** the trees.*

18.3 *At*

This generally refers to places or buildings, but is not used with verbs of movement.

*They arrived **at** the hotel yesterday.*
*I'll see you **at** school.*
*She lives **at** 26, Greet Street.*
*He **went to** the hotel in a taxi.*

18.4 *Behind*

*The broom is **behind** the door.*
*In my driving mirror I can see a huge lorry **behind** me.*

18.5 *Between*

This is used when there are only two things involved.

*He was standing **between** two policemen.*

18.6 *By*

This means 'exactly next to'.

*They live **by** the sea.*

18.7 *In*

This is used with anything which can 'contain' another thing.

*She's **in** the garden.*
*They are **in** the house.*
*He was sitting **in** an armchair.*

It is also used with names of towns and countries, but not with verbs of movement.

*She lives **in** Newcastle.*
*He lives **in** South America.*
*I **went to** Newcastle last month.*

18.8 *In front of*

*I stopped because there was a bus **in front of** me.*

18.9 *Near*

*She lives **near** the park.*
Her house is not far from the park.

18.10 *Next to, next door to*

*Keith usually sits **next to** Jeremy in this lesson.*
*He lives **next door to** me.*

… in the house or room next to mine

18.11 *On*

On generally refers to the 'surface' of an object.

*Put it **on** the table.*

It is also used with these expressions:

*The cinema is **on** the left/right.*
*What's **on** television this evening?*

Which programmes are being shown?

18.12 *Opposite*

*The supermarket is **opposite** the Post Office.*
They are on different sides of the street and face each other.

18.13 *Out/out of*

Out is the opposite of *in*.

*Janet has gone **out**.*   (She is not at home.)
*I had too many apples in my bag and one fell **out**.*

18.14 *To/into*

To describes movement to a place, and needs a verb of movement.

*This morning I walked **to** the shops.*

Into is a combination of *in* and *to*. It describes movement and entering a space which 'contains'.

*She walked **into** the room and everyone stopped talking.*

Compare the use of *at*.

*I arrived **at** the shops before they opened.*

19 Phrasal/multi-word verbs

19.1 Types

1 Verbs with three parts.

*I don't **get on with** my boss.*

The object (*my boss*) has to follow the third part of these verbs.

2 Verbs with two parts and no object.

*I **got up** at six this morning.*

These verbs do not have an object.

3 Verbs with two parts which can be split.

*I **looked up** the answer in my dictionary.*
*I **looked** the answer **up** in my dictionary.*

4 Verbs with two parts which cannot be split.

*Who **looks after** your dog when you are away?*

The object (*your dog*) cannot be put between verb (*looks*) and particle (*after*).

19.2 Problems

It is important to be clear about several things when you learn a new phrasal verb.

1 What type is it? Check with a dictionary.
2 You must learn all of it (two or three words).
3 You must be clear which meaning you are learning, as some of these verbs have more than one meaning.

20 *It* and *there*

There is/are refers to the existence of something.

***There is** a cinema on the corner of the street.*

It refers to something already mentioned.

*There is a cinema on the corner of the street. **It** isn't open on Sunday, though.*

21 List of Irregular Verbs

Infinitive	Past Simple	Past Participle	Infinitive	Past Simple	Past Participle
be	was/were	been	learn	learnt/ed	learnt/ed
beat	beat	beaten	leave	left	left
become	became	become	lend	lent	lent
begin	began	begun	let	let	let
bend	bent	bent	lie	lay	lain
bite	bit	bitten	light	lit	lit
blow	blew	blown	lose	lost	lost
break	broke	broken	make	made	made
bring	brought	brought	mean	meant	meant
build	built	built	meet	met	met
burn	burnt	burnt	pay	paid	paid
buy	bought	bought	put	put	put
catch	caught	caught	read	read	read
choose	chose	chosen	ride	rode	ridden
come	came	come	ring	rang	rung
cost	cost	cost	rise	rose	risen
cut	cut	cut	run	ran	run
deal	dealt	dealt	say	said	said
dig	dug	dug	see	saw	seen
do	did	done	sell	sold	sold
draw	drew	drawn	send	sent	sent
dream	dreamt/ed	dreamt/ed	set	set	set
drink	drank	drunk	shake	shook	shaken
drive	drove	driven	shine	shone	shone
eat	ate	eaten	shoot	shot	shot
fall	fell	fallen	show	showed	shown
feed	fed	fed	shut	shut	shut
feel	felt	felt	sing	sang	sung
fight	fought	fought	sink	sank	sunk
find	found	found	sit	sat	sat
fly	flew	flown	sleep	slept	slept
forbid	forbade	forbidden	speak	spoke	spoken
forget	forgot	forgotten	spell	spelt	spelt
forgive	forgave	forgiven	spend	spent	spent
freeze	froze	frozen	stand	stood	stood
get	got	got	steal	stole	stolen
give	gave	given	stick	stuck	stuck
go	went	gone	swim	swam	swum
grow	grew	grown	take	took	taken
hang	hung	hung	teach	taught	taught
have	had	had	tear	tore	torn
hear	heard	heard	tell	told	told
hide	hid	hidden	think	thought	thought
hit	hit	hit	throw	threw	thrown
hold	held	held	understand	understood	understood
hurt	hurt	hurt	wake	woke	woken
keep	kept	kept	wear	wore	worn
know	knew	known	win	won	won
lay	laid	laid	write	wrote	written
lead	led	led			

INDEX

Functions

Structures

INDEX